The Art of Dominating the Winner's Circle for the College-Minded Student

Anika C. Thrower, Ph.D.

Hues of Health LLC

The Art of Dominating the Winner's Circle for the College-Minded Student

ISBN: 978-1-7321798-2-0

For information regarding special discounts for bulk purchases, instructions on obtaining a free copy for instructional purposes, and/or speaking engagements please contact Hues of Health LLC.

Hues of Health LLC
P.O. Box 7807
New Haven, CT 06519
www.huesofhealth.com

Cover graphic design by Joe Woods

Edited and formatted by Melinda Campbell

Proudly printed in the United States of America

Thank you Jehovah; not once was it ever me.

For those who have sought higher ground for the greater sum, your contribution is appreciated.

Aunt Cat—you will be forever in my heart.

TABLE OF CONTENTS

ACKNOWLEDGEMENT

I stand on the shoulders of my ancestors.

INTRODUCTION

I have always been told that I was nosy. Outside of my own experiences in higher education, I wanted to learn why some students soared through college with flying colors, some struggled, and others simply failed. Throughout my years of teaching, I have built relationships with many college students who journeyed through higher education and won. I find it important to learn something personal about my adult learners. More than anything else, I inquired about their "why." Why did they choose to attend college? Over time I learned, as in my own case, a person's "why" laid the foundation for their success. When an individual's "why" was bigger than themselves, it served as a beacon of hope when the tunnel light was dim, moving them closer to their overarching academic goals.

After carefully studying my students' "whys" and finding the common threads and factors that led to their ultimate success in academia and beyond, I created this book to assist other college-minded students to achieve the same results, using a combination of their predecessors' secret sauce. To clarify, I coined the phrase, "college-minded student," to represent both high school and college students. Solidifying the Winner's Creed, a series of basic keys, as early as possible within academia makes the journey a little less turbulent.

As the title suggests, *The Art of Dominating the Winner's Circle for the College-Minded Student* was written to prepare today's college-minded student to succeed in academia and well beyond. Let me be clear, to be successful in life, a formal college education is not always required. However if making an impact is tucked away in your future plans, then this book will groom you to soar higher fast. Much faster. The keys presented in this book will help to develop the Winner's mindset needed to become responsible stewards of not only ourselves, but our families, our community, our nation, and our world. This book provides some keys to:

- ♟ Understanding our "why"
- ♟ Priming our interpersonal skills
- ♟ Implementing goal setting
- ♟ Honing support systems
- ♟ Developing a manifesto, or personal plan, and *sticking to it*
- ♟ Channeling energy
- ♟ Nurturing the body

Using these keys, I dive into what I call some life hacks and common scenarios students may encounter based on educational levels from high school through graduate school. After reviewing each scenario, the college-minded student is challenged to use the context of the life hack to help a fellow student develop a solution. Don't be surprised if you find a scenario or two that you may have remotely encountered. Each scenario was carefully crafted so that you are able to put your spin on a solution. There is space available to quickly jot down your thoughts. You are encouraged to take the time to solve the scenarios alone or with the help of others. Need further assistance with solving the scenarios?

No worries.

Amongst the many gems planted within the appendixes, you will find suggested answer keys to consider for each and every scenario throughout the book, as well as a Winner's circle manifesto to plan out your weekly priorities, a compilation of the entire Winner's Creed, a compilation of all the motivational affirmations from the book, plus some of my personal favorites.

The journey through higher learning is not always a straight road—it has many unknowns. However, with support and the right mindset it's a road worth traveling.

Do not go it alone, allow this book to be a part of your support system.

A pilot told me that some of the big jet airplanes have a series of blades extending down the wings which cause air to swirl toward the rear of the plane. This provides the necessary turbulence for directional accuracy in flight. If the air is too smooth, some roughness has to be added to improve flight conditions. Perhaps suffering and hardship serve the same purpose for a human being. Maybe we need "turbulence" to help us develop a sense of direction so that we may ultimately reach the destination intended for us in life.

—Norman Vincent Peale

WHY

As youth, most of us are groomed to work hard in order to acquire a job with benefits, raise a family, and buy a home. Each milestone depicts a check mark of success in life. I was no different. Most of us are bombarded by these societal norms and taught to work hard, even at the expense of maintaining our health. At least this is what is portrayed as being normal in many nuclear family households. Over time, I found the strength to quiet the noise from that limiting belief system. After all, life in my younger years threw some pretty ugly curve balls which led me to believe my life here on earth was much bigger than myself.

Family Matriarch

Leading a life as an oblivious high school student came to a screeching halt when devastation struck my family. Because of poor lifestyle choices, I quietly witnessed the passing of two of the most influential women in my life at the prime of theirs—my aunts. This was a delicate time for me, as collectively they stood as the mother figure in my life. In hindsight their premature deaths were directly linked to unhealthy lifestyles, including lack of exercise, excessive alcohol consumption, unmanaged stress, and, most pronounced, poor eating habits. Thinking back to my formative years, I have fond memories of family coming together at rare times such as the holiday seasons. Consider an experience from my personal catalogue of life:

If I closed my eyes tight enough, like yesterday, I could smell the succulent dishes my aunt would prepare during the holiday season. Thanksgiving eve I recall watching attentively as my aunt would prep the festive trimmings, such as chopping the vegetables for her signature homemade cornbread stuffing, ham-hock-seasoned collards, and other southern-inspired side dishes. My aunt fired up the oven in the wee hours of the morning to start her cooking. I would awaken to a home filled with foggy windows accompanied by the intoxicating aromas of the turkey, candied yams, ham, and macaroni and cheese to usher in the day. The competing smells of the dishes danced around her home making everyone happier and giddier by the hour until the feast was finally served.

Being the matriarch of the Thrower family, Aunt Cat truly made the holidays special.

Beyond Formative Beliefs

As I think back I remember my father, a stout man, being physically fit. Outside of having a physically demanding occupation as an electrician, he stayed active. I recall spending many hot summer evenings sitting on the West Park bench watching him play tennis while I slurped on one of Gus's icy ball cups. Also

I remember watching my brother, Abdul, and cousins, Ali and Omar, shooting hoops with their friends at what was the old Allegheny Middle School's basketball court. Modes of physical activity were not new to the people in my family. However, like many families, love, care, and fellowship were oftentimes closely associated with the celebration of food. My family did not consume such a smorgasbord of food as described above on a regular basis, but food made our times together that much more special.

Unknown to me at the time, the scenario I mentioned from my catalogue of life was indicative of socioeconomic status. Because of the daily eating habits and choice of quantity over quality, poor health outcomes are heightened. Research studies and statistical findings show minority populations take the brunt of health calamities. For example, there are a plethora of studies and information which shows strong correlations between poor health status and low educational attainment (e.g., earning a high school diploma or less) remaining a pending concern amongst minority populations.[1] Such factors as unhealthy lifestyles, substandard insurance options, and low-paying wages were predictors of poor health statuses which are indicative of sickness and premature death. As a minority myself, and seeing the effects of poor health within my family, I feared for my own longevity and those people within my community who I mirrored. Cardiovascular disease (CVD) has been the number one cause of death for all Americans for well over a decade, with the highest percentage of deaths unevenly affecting those individuals within minority communities. Moreover, CVD is no longer an ailment which affects only seniors, as today the victims who fall susceptible are getting younger. I have hopes of seeing the tides change on such public health issues— everyone deserves to experience a high quality of life.

Outside of wanting to make a better life for myself, my "why" and how I aspired to make an impact on society was solidified early. It was important to live a life where I could afford to be comfortable. But more importantly, I dreamed of success in life as making conscious decisions to live a higher quality of life, rather than chasing the societal norms that made people susceptible to poor health.

As odd as it sounds, once the gloom cleared regarding the calamities of my formative years, I was able to claim mishaps as veins of empowerment. I embodied a belief system that led me to want to serve people who had an "Aunt Cat" of their own. Because of my background, I believe in a world where higher life expectancies are possible. Those years led me to believe in the possibility of a decrease in the incidence of type 2 diabetes. Through my family's legacy, I believe in less, much less, heart disease. Unbeknown to her,

---

1. National Center for Health Statistics (2017). Health, United States, 2016: With Chartbook on Long-term Trends in Health. Retrieved from https://www.cdc.gov/nchs/data/hus/hus16.pdf#glance
World Health Organization (2017). The Determinants of Health. Retrieved from http://www.who.int/hia/evidence/doh/en/

Aunt Cat strengthened my belief in my ability to have the foresight to want to acquire the skills needed to make an impact well beyond my formative beliefs. But how?

My "why" empowered my journey, which eventually led to my self-induction into *The Art of Dominating the Winner's Circle for the College-Minded Student.*

Education is the most powerful weapon which you can use to change the world.

—Nelson Mandela

WE BELONG

Many pessimists would reason that higher learning or college is not a necessity. However, it's the journey through academia and immersion in the setting that makes the difference. Higher education, along with other experiences during this journey, is the primer to a life of contribution. In other words, the internal work we do on ourselves prepares us for the external work we do in the communities we serve. Within any institute of higher learning, the college-minded student will find other like-minded students from different backgrounds who look and behave quite differently. As much as every college student is different, our interior is the same. The college campus is a breeding ground for a wide range of attributes to be shared, including beliefs and culture. Yet we still have made a calculated choice to define success on individual terms, knowing that through the acquisition of skills, knowledge, and expertise, we are laying the foundation to make a respective impact. We all want to champion for our cause, whether it is the next astronaut who finds a new planet or the teacher who grooms the next world leader to greatness. But more times than none, even the self-motivated college-minded student has fleeting thoughts where our self-worth is questioned.

Do I belong in college?

I was that student. For me, success in academia while in high school was far-fetched. This is because of a lack of role models and my background. There were many times I doubted my ability to obtain success above high school. The thought of attending college classes was intimidating. Being away from the high school friends whom I built bonds with, and in a place full of what I thought to be nothing less than intellectuals, made me doubt my intelligence. I perceived the looks from other students as if they had learned my secret: I was an imposter. Sure I had family members who encouraged me to do well and believed in me. However no amount of words were a match against my own perceived inadequacies. This was nothing new. In fact, as far back as I can remember, I felt inadequate in many facets of my life—beginning my journey in college was no different.

My first year as a student in higher learning was the time in which I experienced the majority of my growing pains. Once the whispers of self-doubt subsided, I learned college was so much more than the monstrous buildings and smiling faces boasted of in the bright brochures. It was at that time that I mentally made the leap from being an unsure young adult to trusting my grown-up intuition, which provided me with the assurance that I was college material.

The fruits of the college campus afforded me the opportunity to consider new perspectives, challenge my respective mindset, and gain knowledge from my professors and fellow students. As I learned how this "college thing" worked, I stayed quiet. Alone-time was used for reflection and concentration on my studies. I knew I was standing on the shoulders of others who came before me. This thought was an immense amount of pressure, yet my formative beliefs fueled me to become hungry for knowledge, study hard, and formulate my perspectives. Based on my major, many of the topics taught and dissected in classes were around health disparities within vulnerable minority populations. These were topics that were subject to be learned by others but relived by me. Individuals living within low income households experience and are prone to develop other relatable disease states. In other words, over time those with type 2 diabetes developed additional chronic ailments to include cancer and/or CVD. Unfortunately, this phenomenon is passed down from generation to generation.

It was important for such topics not to be glossed over. A space for meaningful contributions to such conversations amongst those wanting to make impact on society was required. My silence was broken; I spoke up. I became comfortable being uncomfortable at times and sharing my perspectives on topics of interest with one classmate at a time, then small groups of students before or after class. Like an out-of-body experience, I watched myself shed feelings of inferiority to step into the person I was becoming. In classes full of the *intellects*, I began to assert my voice by making contributions to discussions on a variety of topics, and I even challenged others' perspectives. Through this self-evolution I learned:

♟ My contributions mattered.

♟ Standing on shoulders mandated me to make contributions to those around me.

I began to build alliances and even friendships with my fellow college classmates.

It was in college that I learned the value of seeking associations with people whose actions were conducive to where I was going in my life. The secret sauce was simple: college students who shared similar interests seemed to stick together. For example, athletes trained with other athletes, members of the school band had jam sessions with other band members, and scholars studied with other scholars. By the same token those who partied hung with those who partied, and those who failed seemed to fail together.

As I was immersed in all the tangibles new experiences offered on campus, my education extended beyond the college campus. My formal education in higher learning helped reshape my mindset and create a better version of myself, both inside and (unknown to me at the time) outside of the classroom. As more was expected of me, I expected more from myself—I refused the low-hanging fruit. I wanted to be around friends and family who shared similar values. We, as college-minded students, have the right to *reposition the seating charts in our lives*.

Being a college student confirmed my formative beliefs. It intensified my desire to shorten the gap between wanting to make a difference and actively making an impact. The journey started with me, and once I realized I could make an impact, doors began to open. I learned:

♟ I belong, you belong—we belong.

I have never let my schooling interfere with my education.

—Mark Twain

MOMENTS OF TRUTH

Most people's experience in academia is life changing, to a certain extent. We all have moments of truth. Personally, I equate the scenario to traveling an unfamiliar road and coming to a tunnel:

Entering, the tunnel starts off dimly lit. Once our eyes adjust, we tensely hold the steering wheel with both hands using the best of our driving skills until we adjust to the terrain. Moving forward, and over time, we get our bearings as the once dimly lit road becomes more brilliant. As we are able to realize our journey through the tunnel is coming to an end, we are energized. Regardless of the onset of the blinding glare, we keep moving ahead and out of the tunnel.

Although the experience of traveling the tunnel was uncomfortable, we leave the scenario a better driver. The academic journey is no different—if we are willing to move through the academic journey, we become keenly familiar with each tunnel, valley, hill, mountain, creek, river, and ocean.

My "why" and the impact I wanted to make mandated I rethink my mindset and that of those people I socialized with most often. I critiqued both my voluntary and involuntary interactions within my circle of support. In other words, I learned to question and mastered learning about channeling the energy derived from the people I chose to be around. I questioned interactions and whether or not they were in alignment with my overarching academic goals. There were several moments of truth when I made difficult decisions to cut ties or wean myself away from people. Since iron sharpens iron, I knew I needed to surround myself with the most positive energy conducive to winning.

We inhabit a world full of people. No matter how hard we try to escape interactions and ultimately our reliance on others, life becomes much easier when we cultivate the mindset that we must interact with the right people. Interpersonal skills are worth developing.

Sure there are some lone rangers amongst us, but over the long haul, doing almost everything alone with little interaction with others becomes counterproductive. Outside of family and well established friends, there is no way around minimal contact with other people, such as college professors, fellow students, and those people we consider to be a part of the circle of support in our lives. Dominating the Winner's circle requires us to do the *heart* work of building and cultivating relationships both in and out of the college setting.

Moments of truth that build sustainable relationships come in spurts and are rarely convenient. They come about based upon our reaction to these scenarios in relation to our own lives, rather than the actual scenario itself. The silver lining is that while on our journey to higher learning, the college–minded student has an opportunity to grow in each scenario encountered while practicing *balance*. By thoughtfully handling each scenario, we strengthen our interpersonal skills. Consider this thought: if we learn early on how to navigate through common college-minded life hacks for higher learning, we can develop a winning edge. This draws us closer to our "why" and the ability to make an impact. Learning common life hacks makes our journey much smoother. Embracing moments of truth helps us on our path to winning.

The Winner's Creed

- Winners learn most people's experience in academia is life changing, to a certain extent.
- Winners learn that iron sharpens iron—surround ourselves with the most positive energy conducive to winning.
- Winners learn moments of truth that build sustainable relationships come in spurts and are rarely convenient.
- Winners learn that by thoughtfully handling each scenario, we strengthen our interpersonal skills.

The most important single ingredient in success is knowing how to get along with people.

—Theodore Roosevelt

PAYING DUES

Usually our education before college suggests how well we will do in college. Success in high school heightens the probability of successful outcomes in higher learning. This is because it is difficult to suddenly cultivate ambition in the latter part of a youth's high school education. The average non-studious student must become tenacious to gain the skills required to succeed in college. But if dominance in the Winner's circle is the goal, it can be done! In other words, the once mediocre student can cultivate success.

In high school I considered myself an average student with an average mindset. Studying and achieving high marks were unimportant. I just wanted to be done. While in high school, I was always shocked when I got an A or B on my report card. I wondered how it happened, assuming either the teacher made a mistake or just liked me. I didn't equate these grades with the quality of work I produced. I did not believe in my ability to do well in high school. It was not until my late teens and the passing of my aunts that I felt it was possible to stand for something bigger than myself and make an impact on society.

To dominate the Winner's circle, no one is exempt from paying dues. We pay now or pay later. Simply put, we all must work hard now or work hard later to achieve the goals in our lives. Paying dues means being willing to do what it takes in academia to acquire the skills, knowledge, and expertise needed to make the maximum impact. Based on my decisions in life, I "paid later." For me, it was difficult to build the skills needed to become studious and succeed in college, or even approach college with the right mindset. I doubted myself. I learned as I went through a rough patch or (figuratively) approached an unfamiliar tunnel to allow myself time to pause and review my goals. It was in those times that my "why" was not only reignited but also strengthened.

Similar to my experience, the average freshman college student will find stepping foot onto the college campus overwhelming. It is easy to get lost in the hustle and bustle of all the other seemingly confident students walking to and fro. However, the curious student quickly learns that college is an institution that caters to the college-minded student (which we will discuss in a moment), regardless of one's age, race, ethnicity, gender, sexual orientation or disability. College doors swing wide open for the ambitious student with the desire to win in higher learning. Those who flunk out of college do so for a few reasons. They lack:

- ♟ Self-efficacy
- ♟ Precision to plan and set goals
- ♟ Being around like-minded energy
- ♟ Willingness to pay dues

11

Early on we must take the time to ask ourselves questions to figure out how to align our personal belief system, the impact we want to make, and academic goals.

Before paying dues we must set the target or the goals we envision accomplishing and aim with precision. Our stores of energy are not limitless, therefore without planning, we are unable to effectively direct our best efforts on what we were meant to accomplish in higher learning. We tend to get sidetracked with all the small smoke screens in life. Developing strategies to take ownership in our journey develops accountability and keeps our "why" in plain view. Be willing to reach back in history and do the *heart* work of digging within ourselves to learn our "why" and our purpose.

Ponder on your "why" and complete Exercise 1. Based on your "why" and staying away from fine details, briefly describe how making an impact on yourself and others would look:

Exercise 1: Your "Why"

_____

_____

_____

_____

_____

_____

_____

_____

_____

_____

Taking time to discover the life we want to live and our "why" is an important task. For some, the answer will come naturally. Pondering on this question and discovering the answer will save the college-minded student time, energy, and money. Staying aware of our "why" predicts our goals in higher learning and well beyond and gives us an idea of what it takes to obtain the degree we desire. The college-minded students who have found and dominated the winning edge learned the road was worth traveling.

The Winner's Creed

- Winners learn that success in high school heightens the probability of successful outcomes in higher learning.
- Winners learn we pay now or pay later.
- Winners learn college doors swing wide open for the ambitious student with the desire to win in higher learning.
- Winners learn developing strategies to take ownership in our journey develops accountability and keeps our "why" in plain view.

The thing about paying your dues is that you're not the one who sets the price.

—Alan Robert Neal

SPEAKING OF DEGREES

The era of enrolling into college and then going with the flow to figure things out on the fly is over. Times have changed. Today's brick-and-mortar college campus has everything we need to achieve academic success. A college campus has all the bells and whistles to cater to the college-minded student, including financial aid, student life counselors, administrative supports, advisors, study service centers, tutorial labs, health centers, libraries, student clubs, professors, and fellow students.

There are many disciplines that a person can study and obtain various levels of education in, depending on the dues we are willing to pay. Examples of degrees and average periods of obtainment include:

- Associate's degree in a field of choice (2–2.5 years)
- Bachelor's degree in a field of choice (Additional 2–3 years above an associate's degree or 4–5 years)
- Master's degree in field of choice (Additional 2–3 years above a bachelor's degree)
- Doctoral degree in a field of choice (Additional 3–10 years above a master's degree)

Unsurprisingly the more knowledge, expertise, specialized training and credentials desired will determine how much time we should be ready to devote to our college journey. Furthermore, the higher the level of education one pursues, the more rigorous the curriculum becomes. To illustrate, someone whose ultimate goal is to become a board-certified physician must ground himself to embark on a strict curriculum, several years of specialized training as a medical student and then completion of a residency.

There are thousands of roads college-minded students can travel that will lead them to achieving their goals in higher learning.

Outside of the customary college campus, the World Wide Web makes it possible for almost anyone to get a degree. Equipped with a computer and an internet connection, a degree can be obtained remotely from anywhere around the world. Within the last few decades, fully accredited online institutions have become a viable source of higher learning. In the world of technology, obtaining a degree of choice in higher learning has become a reality for thousands upon thousands of students who introduced themselves into the art of dominating the Winner's circle for the college-minded student. Considering an online college education is worth exploring for those of us who are well organized, can work independently, and are committed to working hard.

By obtaining a degree, whether at a brick-and-mortar institution or online, we are able to pursue our studies at our own pace. This means after reviewing our goals, we can go as fast or as slow as we prefer. For those who choose to travel the academic journey at a slower pace or pursue their studies part-time because of life circumstances, that's okay. Personally, I admire the adult learner who has made a path where there was none. We should not count out the determined untraditional student. They understand there is no expiration date on obtaining the requirements needed to obtain a degree or in essence pay dues. They have not only found a way to win but also to dominate the Winner's circle by understanding their limitations and in spite of them making plans to win.

Some students, out of necessity, may need to take a pause and drop down from being a full-time student to a part-time student. In these instances we must be careful to stick to the plan of not losing sight of our "why," watching a dim light flicker and die. Always remember being either a part-time or full-time student equals being an enrolled student. Here are a few quick life hacks to stay the course regardless of enrollment status:

- Be willing to evaluate sources of energy and the quality of the interactions within our circle of support.
- Do not wait for others to believe in our own belief system.
- When we don't believe in our own ability, believe in our possibility.
- Write down goals and review them often.

The Winner's Creed

- Winners learn today's brick-and-mortar college campus has everything we need to achieve academic success.
- Winners learn the higher the level of education one pursues, the more rigorous the curriculum becomes.
- Winners learn after reviewing our goals, we can go as fast or as slow as we prefer.

Whatever the mind can conceive and believe, it can achieve.

—Napoleon Hill

SEEKING SUPPORT

Some may wonder if goals in higher learning can feel far-fetched. Undeniably, yes. The bigger the goal the crazier it could and absolutely should look. Taking the leap from high school to college can seem especially daunting when we feel there is a lack of role models in our field of study. Seek them! It is well worth the effort to find them locally and beyond, as they want to be sought.

Though their time could be limited, many role models within our community are flattered to mentor others, as they too were probably mentored at some point. When approaching these successful people we want to associate with more often, the spirit of meekness goes a long way. Think of making direct connection through a concise email, phone call or handwritten letter. Upon lines of communication being open, if we are willing to align our schedules with their availability and promise to use a small amount of their time, they may quickly accommodate our request. Most likely our local role models are willing to have a discussion over a cup of coffee or a quick bite to eat. For the Winner's edge, before the meeting find a topic you and your role model may have in common, whether it be professional or a hobby. Know as much about them as possible. This may be a great way to build rapport and soften the lead into a conversation about our special interest. Those in the Winner's circle show value for their time by being concise about what you want to discuss and ending the conversation as agreed. These kinds of interpersonal skills will lead to our role model being open to meet again. Also they may consider us as a new connection, next time seeking us. Never underestimate the power of making an inquiry.

Local high school and college campuses alike have a wealth of resources available at our disposal. For example, an up-and-coming college-minded student who sees herself in a life of politics may be surprised to learn she has connections with influential political figures, once she becomes familiar with the school's alumni directory. A senior journalist for the college newspaper looking to land her first job may learn through inquiries that she has a link to an influential connection with a citywide newspaper in her area of interest. Many times our role model is a phone call away. Building our interpersonal skills goes a long way.

Each time we reach out to make contact with a seemingly successful person, it either gets easier or we are pointed in a more resourceful direction. The college-minded student is careful not to be deterred or allow local resources to go untapped.

Many times through the network of people we associate with most, someone could lead us to the connection we desire. Pulling out our list of associates/friends may go far. These connections are just another reason to surround ourselves with others who are goal-oriented. Those in the Winner's circle are always willing to use the resourcefulness of the people around them. And for those role models who are distant, remember successful people leave clues. Follow their careers. Research their work. Read their blogs. Read their books. Join the groups they are in online. For those college-minded students who are willing to do the research, we have full access to a role model's journey, at least through the internet.

The college-minded student learns how to seek the support of others and also knows that our interpersonal skills are traits worth developing early. Pursuing and cultivating a support system in academia that inspires us to live a life of contribution pushes us forward not only in high school and college but well beyond. If we dare to start early we will acquire the skill of handpicking those traits in ourselves and others that challenge us to be our best selves. More importantly, as we benefit from the support of others, we are well positioned to show our gratitude by lending a hand and being of service to others within our circle of support and elsewhere.

The Winner's Creed

- ♟ Winners learn the bigger the goal the crazier it could and absolutely should look.
- ♟ Winners learn to never underestimate the power of making an inquiry.
- ♟ Winners learn how to seek the support of others and also know that our interpersonal skills are traits worth developing early.
- ♟ Winners learn to lend a hand and be of service to others within our circle of support and elsewhere.

Each one teach one.

—African American Proverb

PLANNING AROUND OTHER PEOPLE

No matter how we choose to fill our time, everyone has the same amount allotted to them. One day equals 24 hours or 1,440 minutes. This means every one of us gets the same 604,800 seconds in a week. At first glance this may seem like a huge amount of time to accomplish our goals in academia. Actually, it is not as much time as we think, once we factor in other necessary activities. After we account for such necessaries as sleep, each one of us is guilty at one time or another of being susceptible to time-squandering. In other words, we often allow the people closest to us or even ourselves to mismanage our time. In order to dominate the Winner's circle the college-minded student must not misuse a single second. How might time-squandering look?

- Checking the internet for specific information that turns into hours of internet surfing
- Answering a quick incoming phone call that turns into hours of idle conversation

Time-management-based life hacks can help us use our time wisely and accomplish our overarching academic goals. The notion that we have all day to accomplish something can derail our goals. I am not suggesting that every day should have a rigorous schedule, but we should plan each day with at least one specific goal. For example, if we need to study, have dinner plans, or simply need to get laundry done, we should plan and follow through. This keeps us focused on our "why" and keeps our ultimate goals unconditional. Momentarily we will discuss developing a manifesto, or personal plan. Part of planning means considering our interpersonal relationships and defining how other people and their needs fit into our lives.

We have all had those friends within our circle of support who ask for a small favor, promising to use only a small amount of time. Harmless enough, right? Though good-natured, sometimes what was supposed to take a few moments of our time turned into several moments, hours, or sometimes full days. Having relationships in our everyday lives can leave us susceptible to helping and supporting other people as they too support us.

On a case-by-case basis we have to ask ourselves if we really have the flexibility in our schedule to support others' requests. Emergencies are always exceptions, but we may have to set boundaries around what we can and cannot do. When last-minute requests are made of us from friends, it is OK to tactfully decline (as warranted). If possible, we may help, but we should be honest about our intentions of when we can assist. After reviewing our schedule of short-term goals, consider coming up with another permissible time. Then communicate that day and time as soon as possible. On their end, if it's important enough and they cannot wait, they will seek help from others. Friends may be a little disappointed about the lack of expediency on our part, however true friends will respect our boundaries. Be mindful as college-minded students ourselves, we must provide the same level of consideration.

Outside of being honest about time constraints, when we are finally in the moment with the friend as promised, we are likely to be more attentive to their needs. Friends are especially delighted if we are able to use the life hack of *under-promising but over-delivering*. To illustrate, we promise to help a friend study for a test on Sunday morning (which is several days away) but after reviewing our plans we see an earlier day and time is available to assist much sooner, thus *under-promising but over-delivering*. This tactic is especially effective on our academic journey to keep integrity with ourselves and retain valuable connections to our circle of support.

Seeking and cultivating high-quality relationships over quantity helps to curtail many issues we may have with other people, as these fellow Winners stay connected to both their "why" and *our* "why."

The Winner's Creed

- ♟ Winners learn the notion that we have all day to accomplish something can derail our goals.
- ♟ Winners learn that having relationships in our everyday lives can leave us susceptible to helping and supporting other people as they too support us.
- ♟ Winners learn when last-minute requests are made of us from friends, it is OK to tactfully decline (as warranted).
- ♟ Winners learn that friends may be a little disappointed about the lack of expediency on our part, however true friends will respect our boundaries.
- ♟ Winners learn to use the life hack of *under-promising but over-delivering*.

If you fail to plan, you are planning to fail.

—Benjamin Franklin

BREAKS AND REWARD SYSTEMS

The college-minded student needs to be mindful that life happens. The life hack of taking a pause or break at these times does not mean we have lost sight of our goals, rather taking a momentary break helps us remain affixed to our "why." We all need breaks at some point to unwind and regroup. It is much more effective to be proactive about taking breaks than to have to wreck an ambitious schedule because we have hit a physical or mental wall.

Early on in our college journey we should become familiar with both the mental health and student life services available on campus. These college-based resources employ caring staff, who specialize in assisting students to sort through feelings, issues, and problems. They are qualified to recommend next steps. Allowing issues to linger without seeking help will make problems multiply. Those students in the Winner's circle understand the importance of using discernment to seek help.

A break could look different to different people, based on one's individual circumstances. Taking care of ourselves should be our highest priority. To illustrate, think of the need to get routine maintenance on a car. When we take our car in for service, we allow a qualified technician to check the various systems in our car, including the transmission system, braking system, engine, tires, etc. What would happen if we continue to put off such routine car maintenance and leave these essential systems unchecked? The same holds true for ourselves.

Ideas on how to take a break could include a long conversation with a friend from our circle of support, exercise, catching a movie, and/or even rejuvenating with a nap. Such pauses are good around periods of high stress, such as studying for final exams and managing sudden life-altering events. No one is immune to the unforeseen, and the timing of these experiences is always awful. Sickness and/or deaths in our lives cannot be anticipated, even with our best planning skills. In those instances, let us be gentle on ourselves and believe in the power of finding the time to take a break, to exhale. Unfortunately, there tends to be a stigma around seeking mental health services. College campuses provide mental health services, which should be a part of one's support system. This consideration is healthy and keeps Winners on their path to winning.

Outside of unforeseen breaks, developing the life hack of a reward system allows us to deliberately etch time into our schedule to remove ourselves from the hustle and bustle of our ambitious schedule and practice self-care. We can use our reward system when we complete a large project or do well in some other respect. These moments away from our rigid schedules serve as a protection to prevent mental fatigue and keep our mindset strong. Rewards do not have to be attached to monetary value and ideas are endless. They could include time for leisure reading, an extended weekend, time away from the campus to watch a movie with a friend, or just some time alone. Lastly, a reward system gives us something to look forward to as we are in the midst of our busy lives. Unless there is an emergency, resist the urge to use the time allotted for our reward system to push someone else's agenda. At all cost avoid such self-talk as, "Oh, I can go to the movies anytime," or "It's not really important to go to the gym today." Hold and honor the space we leave for ourselves.

Lastly one person's reward system could look totally different from another's reward system. Balance is vital for the college-minded student. The art of dominating the Winner's circle for the college-minded student means balancing our lives by carving breaks and reward systems into our schedules.

The Winner's Creed

- ♟ Winners learn taking a momentary break helps us remain affixed to our "why."
- ♟ Winners learn pauses are good around periods of high stress, such as studying for final exams and managing sudden life-altering events.
- ♟ Winners learn sickness and/or deaths in our lives cannot be anticipated, even with our best planning skills.
- ♟ Winners learn a reward system gives us something to look forward to as we are in the midst of our busy lives.

There is virtue in work and there is virtue in rest. Use both and overlook neither.

—Alan Cohen

DEVELOPING A MANIFESTO

We occupy a world where technology is everywhere. With the swipe of a few fingertips on our smartphones we can manage our busy schedules via syncing calendars and setting alerts. Our phones can manage our entire lives. Try to resist the urge to use these quick fixes when possible.

There is a special magic that becomes apparent when we develop a personal habit of using old-fashioned pen and paper to write down our goals. Keeping mental notes or quickly jotting things down on a loose piece of paper is fine to a certain extent for casual activities. However, to accomplish our goals in academia, we need to make use of an organized system to stay accountable to ourselves. This paper-based system will keep us in alignment with all of our commitments. This includes attending classes, managing study time with cohorts, reviewing class notes, and meeting with professors or other college personnel. Outside of college we need to fulfill community-based obligations, attend to domestic duties, network, and socialize. Because life happens (even in college), we also have to be sure we are taking into account a reward system.

Cultivating the practice of being organized and building a written daily manifesto, or personal plan, to manage our college schedule allows us to keep a running record of all our goals. This running record provides a way to literally look back at our goals whenever necessary to assess progress and make adjustments as needed. Reviewing our goals moves us closer to our wins, class by class, semester by semester, and year by year.

It is important to consider timing when creating our short-term (i.e., daily or weekly) personal manifesto for accomplishing our goals in higher learning. A systematic way of planning is an underrated life hack that moves us over time to our long-term goals. When planning, it is important to consider the times of day during which we are most productive. This concept gives the college-minded student the winning edge. This will vary from person to person. Consider the schedules of Sebastian, Madelyn and Zolia. Each a college student who takes the time to develop their schedule based on their personal preferences:

- ♟ Sebastian is a self-proclaimed night owl. He is able to have a productive day and thrive during the latter part of the night. People like Sebastian find it helpful to create a daily personal manifesto the night before. In that way, an assessment of the activities he accomplished that day are fresh in his mind and he can plan his next day. Additionally, it takes the chore out of thinking about his daily tasks early the next morning. Since Sebastian is not a morning person, having a written manifesto upon waking allows him to hit the ground running the next day.

♟ Madelyn is a morning person. She sees the early hours as a time to thrive. People like Madelyn prefer to use the quieter moments of the day to be still and mindful. Coupled with meditation, an hour-long walk (most mornings), and her coffee, being mindful and planning go hand in hand. Powered by a well rested mind, Madelyn is able to move into her day with ease.

♟ Zolia is a weekend warrior (yes, they are people too). People like her seem to be able to get a lot of tasks accomplished on the weekends with ease. Zolia takes delight in building her personal manifesto at the beginning of the week, especially on Sunday. It is this time that allows Zolia to be mindful of the full week's goals and objectives at one point in time, instead of in pieces over several days during the week. Zolia admits that planning in this manner is more time-consuming but it takes the work out of planning daily and she can occupy that time otherwise. Equipped with the willingness to make changes as priorities change works in Zolia's favor.

Sebastian, Madelyn, and Zolia have each designated a time for planning their busy college schedules. Each found organized routines and life hacks that work for their lifestyles. The best way to determine the most productive part of our day is to simply start planning and note the times that work best. Through trial and error, Winners stay mindful of the most mentally agile moments of the day.

For an easy reference, consider keeping a paper-based calendar accessible at all times as a way to make a quick reference and keep track of goals. A preference of many students in higher learning is to tuck their calendars into a backpack. The college-minded student has several types of calendars of different sizes to choose from: monthly, weekly, and daily. In this way, full pages are available with the ability to assign activities by the hour, each hour of the day. For example, for a study-group-based activity we may write the activity, "study group," in the spaces between 7 p.m. to 9 p.m. For emphasis, some college students use a colored highlighter to etch blocks around the respective activity.

Ranking by Priority Method

For the winning edge, consider adding one additional layer to the manifesto. To ensure that we correctly prioritize our activities, label the importance of the activities, especially during stressful time periods such as finals. This could happen by using the Ranking by Priority Method to prioritize activities (see Figure 1). The Ranking by Priority Method works because inadvertently on any given day, especially when the stakes are high, we have all said in our minds (over and over again) what we have to accomplish as a way to keep a goal alive. For example, as we go about our day we tell ourselves such things as "I have to study after my last class." Why not give ourselves the Winner's edge and heighten our odds of remembering by writing such things down? This would keep us accountable and organized while potentially removing a layer of anxiety.

Figure 1: Ranking by Priority Method

I Must	I Can	I Wish
There is no wiggle room in the timing of this activity—it takes priority. **Example:** Study for calculus exam	This activity is relatively important, but it could be prioritized for another day soon. **Example:** Laundry	It would be great to complete this task, but it could be put on the back burner for a leisure day. **Example:** Lunch with friends

Content of a manifesto will vary from student to student based on lifestyle and respective priorities. Using the Ranking by Priority Method, let us review Janet's manifesto for a Wednesday compared to that for a Saturday.

Because she is taking five classes this semester, her weekday manifesto is much more rigid (see Figure 2). This week her Wednesday is comprised of 3 "I Must" activities. Outside of "I Must" activities, "I Can" will be attending a late-evening study group, while activities like laundry and lunch with a classmate would be "I Wish" activities.

Unlike her weekday schedule, Janet's Saturday manifesto would be relaxed (see Figure 3). She knows the importance of recharging with a reward system. She would have "I Must" activities denoted but on the more relaxed side to include doing laundry, getting some physical activity, and going to the campus arcade with her friends. Her "I Can" activity would be lunch with a buddy. Studying would be on the "I Wish"-based activity.

Figure 2: Janet's Wednesday Manifesto

I Must	I Can	I Wish
3 Classes	Evening study group (1.5 hours)	Laundry
Scheduled meeting with biology professor (30 minutes)		Lunch with a classmate
Band practice (1.5 hours)		

Figure 3: Janet's Saturday Manifesto

I Must	I Can	I Wish
Laundry (2 hours)	Lunch with a buddy (1 hour)	Studying (1 hour)
Physical activity (1 hour)		
Arcade with friends (2 hours)		

Consider how best to use the Ranking by Priority Method as a means to practice the notion that less is more. This means not weighing down one's manifesto and respecting time. Use the cushion method by scheduling more time than needed. For example, if a study group is expected to last 1.5 hours, schedule 2 hours to account for potential unforeseen time overage (e.g., late start time). Being flexible by using this cushion method saves hurriedness and feelings of overwhelm.

The essence of perfecting time-management basics allows the college-minded student to decide priorities for any given day and, using ranking, assign timed activities. Ultimately learning and consistently using time-management basics to complete each task promotes balance. Balance cultivates self-care while allowing us to keep integrity with our limited stores of time and energy.

How might this look?

Let us look back at Janet's Saturday manifesto. The college-minded student would do well to allot enough time to comfortably complete each task. Physical activity will be done first thing in the morning. Next would be laundry, which may entail sorting, washing, drying, and folding clothes. Sure, while the clothes are washing and drying it's tempting to try to catch up on social media statuses and sift through emails. Inadvertently, in some cases this type of multitasking can lead to feelings of connectedness and short-term gratification but also overwhelm.

Using some basics we learned through Janet's manifesto, use the same Ranking by Priority Method and take a few moments to use the Winner's Circle Manifesto planted in the back of the book to rank your own activities. (See Appendix A.)

Lastly, let's put our knowledge to work by helping to develop a Sunday manifesto for both Scott and CJ. They are roommates in college with very different priorities and lifestyles.

Roommate 1 Scenario: Scott is a college senior athlete and has many performance-based awards under his belt for football. He is the lead quarterback on the school's Division I football team. For him, Sundays were made for rest and relaxation. Today is Sunday, let's help Scott plan out his day. It may be useful to know Scott feels he has studied enough over the last several days—besides he reasons he needs only a C average to maintain his sports scholarship. In addition, he admits that outside of his friends on the football team, his relationships have suffered and he wants to strengthen personal bonds with others. How might Scott's Sunday manifesto look?

Within Exercise 2, use the choice of activities below to help Scott choose 4 activities to do on Sunday. First indicate the tasks that should be completed by putting an X on the line in front of the tasks you select for Scott. Then use the Ranking by Priority Method as a way to rank each activity. To do this, affix the corresponding number of importance on each line at the end of the activity selected to represent:

      1: I Must (activity takes priority)

      2: I Can (activity could be prioritized for another day soon)

      3: I Wish (activity could be put on the back burner for an upcoming leisure day)

Again, select ONLY 4 activities. All activities listed will not be used. Lastly, based on Scott's background and what you understand about his priorities, provide some reasoning about the choices selected. After completing this assignment check the back of the book for more insight (see Appendix B).

Exercise 2: Scott's Activity Choices

Choose Task	Activity	Rank Importance
	Participate in a study group (1.5 hours)	
	Revisit notes from the week's classes (1 hour)	
	Complete a cardiovascular workout (1 hour)	
	Attend church (2 hours)	
	Grab brunch with a high school buddy (1.5 hours)	
	Watch an animal-based documentary (3 hours)	
	Go grocery shopping (1 hour)	
	Check in with parents (30 minutes)	
	Register for fall classes online (15 minutes)	
	Do laundry (1.5 hours)	

Reasoning for Scott's Sunday Personal Manifesto

_____

_____

_____

_____

_____

_____

_____

_____

_____

Roommate 2 Scenario: CJ, a college sophomore, has been coined as a scholar and is attending on a full academic scholarship. For him, Sundays mean digging into his studies without the hassle of attending classes. Today is Sunday, so let's help CJ plan out his day. It may be useful to know that CJ is a perfectionist and takes pride in having been on the Dean's List each semester. He knows he has been slacking on caring for himself but reasons that his attending college is contingent on maintaining high grades. He has hopes of being a veterinarian one day. How might CJ's Sunday manifesto look?

Within Exercise 3, use the choice of activities below to help CJ choose 4 activities to do on Sunday. First indicate the tasks that should be completed by putting an X on the line in front of the tasks you select for CJ. Then use the Ranking by Priority Method as a way to rank each activity. To do this, affix a corresponding number of importance on each line at the end of the activity selected to represent:

> 1: I Must (activity takes priority)
>
> 2: I Can (activity could be prioritized for another day soon)
>
> 3: I Wish (activity could be put on the back burner for an upcoming leisure day)

Again, select ONLY 4 activities. All activities listed will not be used. Lastly, based on CJ's background and what you understand about his priorities, provide some reasoning about the choices selected. After completing this assignment check the back of the book for more insight (see Appendix C).

Exercise 3: CJ's Activity Choices

Choose Task	Activity	Rank Importance
	Participate in a study group (1.5 hours)	
	Revisit notes from the week's classes (1 hour)	
	Complete a cardiovascular workout (1 hour)	
	Attend church (2 hours)	
	Grab brunch with a high school buddy (1.5 hours)	
	Watch an animal-based documentary (3 hours)	
	Go grocery shopping (1 hour)	
	Check in with parents (30 minutes)	
	Register for fall classes online (15 minutes)	
	Do laundry (1.5 hours)	

Reasoning for CJ's Sunday Personal Manifesto:

_____

_____

_____

_____

_____

_____

_____

_____

_____

_____

When college-minded students develop a personal manifesto and execute the plan daily, we build an internal accountability system within ourselves that keeps us affixed to our "why."

As a final point, be mindful that one's schedule should reflect quality over quantity. For both Scott and CJ, less meant more. In other words, an endless list of activities does not necessarily reflect productivity. Let's face it, with all the moving parts and responsibilities we must juggle, being a college student is a job. Balance and fostering time-management skills will lead to the college-minded student winning time after time and ultimately dominating the Winner's circle.

The Winner's Creed

- Winners learn cultivating the practice of being organized and building a written daily manifesto, or personal plan, to manage our college schedule allows us to keep a running record of all our goals.
- Winners learn through trial and error to stay mindful of the most mentally agile moments of the day.
- Winners learn balance cultivates self-care while allowing us to keep integrity with our limited stores of time and energy.

Goals are the links in the chain that connect activity to accomplishment.

—Tom Ziglar

LIFE HACKS FOR CHANNELING ENERGY

Before we explore the concept of channeling energy, let us complete an exercise where we take a good look at ourselves. We all have traits that bring energy and are seen as admirable by others. For example, in high moments of stress we may be the level-headed one. Whereas another person may have the gift of gab and can get along with almost anyone. For Exercise 4, think of 2 or more ways you bring your most positive energy to others when you are at your best:

Exercise 4: Your Energy

_____

_____

_____

_____

For this next exercise, without straining, take several moments to think of your current circle of support and how each individual indirectly adds value to your life. With that thought in mind for Exercise 5, name 2 people you associate with most and outline ways they bring their most positive energy to you when they are at their best:

Exercise 5: Others' Energy

_____

_____

_____

_____

For Exercise 4 were you surprised at what you discovered about yourself? Did your best self come to mind with ease?

If completing Exercise 5 was easy, good. If it caused strain, even better. This is because we always have the opportunity to take as much energy or as little energy as we choose from those people we consider to be our circle of support. Whether we suffer from low-quality energy relationships or we lack bonds with the right people, it's time to consider some life hacks to detect, and draw closer to, the energy that is conducive to our plans to successfully complete college. In fact, bonding with progressive people, who have positive energy a majority of the time, is more than half the battle to dominate the Winner's circle.

As a last point, did you find that you and some people within your circle of support shared some of the same traits? There is a saying, "opposites attract." This could be true in some respects. But as college-minded students, when we are dealing with our future and making an impact, we are responsible for our relationships. This means extracting those traits from others which have a progressive nature or at least harmonize with our respective energy.

All people have energy. Think about it—we have all had a casual conversation at one time or another with a stranger that has left us thinking about the interaction well after the conversation concluded. For example, if the conversation was about a common hobby, mutually enjoyed, we would have probably been enticed to stay in the moment longer. Being in such a space with these sparks of high energy allow for an intellectual exchange of information and ideas. All interactions between family, friends, and/or fellow students exchange energy that results in growth or deterioration. Growth and deterioration cannot occupy the same environment. No matter the kind of energy we receive from others, with the right mindset, we always have an opportunity to use our interpersonal skills to at least spread positive energy.

Up until this point, as adults, the sources of energy we have positioned ourselves in have been byproducts of what was created for us or allowed to grow and cultivate in our daily lives. In our formative years, we did not have many choices (or the ability to exercise our choice) of how our time was spent and who we were around. Being on the cusp of adulthood, we now have more choices. Being a college-minded student means we now have a new level of responsibility for ourselves about our surroundings. We no longer have to subject ourselves to unproductive energy.

To illustrate, let's consider the lay of the land, or circumstances, with a scenario between junior college classmates Thomas and Joe.

Lay of the Land: The midterm exam is scheduled for today. Equipped with his coffee, Thomas arrives to class an hour early to review notes. For the winning edge, he has hopes of last-minute connections with other ambitious students from his study group. When he looks up from reviewing his notes, he sees Joe dragging himself through the door. Regardless of previous negative energy from his friend, Thomas hopes for the best and takes a gamble on opening a conversation.

31

Scenario: *Thomas: Hello, Joe, great to see you. How was your weekend?*

Joe: (sigh) Could have been better. Today is Monday and you know how I feel about Mondays...my roommate snores all night long...my team lost last night...I hear it's supposed to rain today...(after 25 minutes of whining)...hey Luz mentioned we are having an exam today, is that true?

What can we get from this scenario? Sure, Thomas should be honored that Joe feels comfortable enough to confide in him, but Thomas paid a price. His time was squandered. Unknown to Thomas, his classmate is a habitual complainer who used the time for a cynical interaction. For Joe, it is difficult to be enthusiastic when life appears to have more downs than ups. Hopefully Thomas was able to compartmentalize this interaction and do well on the exam, but Joe may be a different story. If Joe does not realign his energy, nothing will go right for him. He will continue to unconsciously seek others willing to fuel his somber disposition that only feeds his pessimistic energy.

It is natural to vent. We all have our moments. Nonetheless the college-minded student must be careful not to allow such an unproductive mindset to squander our time. We are entitled to surround ourselves with the best energy possible. Furthermore, the game changer is being able to ignite our own energy or at least guard our energy. Let's revisit the scenario between Joe and Thomas. Notice the energy channeling life hack Thomas could have used:

Lay of the Land: The midterm exam is scheduled for today. Equipped with his coffee, Thomas arrives to class an hour early to review notes. When he looks up, he sees Joe dragging himself through the door. Since he must stay on task, he knows he must keep the communication brief.

Scenario: *Thomas: (looks up and smiles) Good morning, Joe.*

Joe: Good morning.

Thomas inhales another sip of coffee and quickly gets back to the task of reviewing his notes.

We have all known organized people like Thomas who had the right stuff to succeed but failed because of their associations with the wrong people, like Joe. A life hack that well organized college-minded students use is making it our business to expose ourselves to the right circles of support. Know when to stay away from such people as Joe. In this way, we can always expect successful outcomes in higher learning because we are amongst Winners.

Let's step away from this scenario and consider various types of energy we get from people and within our environment.

Positive Energy

Positive energy feels good and can be derived from our environment. Most of us have found ourselves wanting to be in certain places that uplift us or have positive vibes—just because. A life hack that many students use is hibernating in the college campus library. If the sight of the monstrous amounts of books were not enough, without touching a single page of one of the thousands of books at our disposal, we extract other riches, such as freedom from distractions and most importantly the telepathic energy from the other students determined to win. Surely the books do not have any magical powers, rather it is the ambiance the library provides which propels the college-minded student forward. For big wins in academia, positive energy should be reflective in the places we frequent most often.

To illustrate further, consider an experience from my personal catalogue of life:

Through living on both coasts and frequent travel in between, I have found a worldwide chain of coffee houses (which will remain nameless) particularly appealing. Frequenting these establishments has been my life hack. Outside of enjoying the coffee, I have encountered worthwhile interactions through exchanging a smile, chatting about the weather, or informally talking about a current event. For me, woven into these coffee houses, were other people like me. From what I could gather, they were just as determined to pay dues on their terms. Coupled with coffee, I enjoyed the aura of other Winners. The barista's demeanor has been an experience in itself. I have never inquired but I can only assume either the baristas were vetted before hire for innate, upbeat personalities and/or they go through thorough customer service training. Whatever the case I feel as if each occasion I have visited the establishment, the barista's only mission in life was to carefully brew me that perfect cup of coffee.

Outside of the energy we can get from a place or individuals like the barista mentioned, positive energy could come from a particular individual who has neither a big voice nor extraordinary qualities but who indirectly raises our energy levels. Think of encouraging vibes that we may get from a casual acquaintance. There is no substitute for being around uplifting individuals who aspire to positively impact others and themselves. Since growth and deterioration cannot occupy the same environment, seeking and retaining bonds with positive people who have ambition wins hands down every time. As a word of caution, positive energy may not always feel warm and fuzzy. This type of energy should organically push us out of our comfort zone at some points to come more fully into our best selves.

Next let us consider another type of energy which many times college-minded students see as harmless—neutral energy.

Neutral Energy

Neutral energy can be detrimental to our progression in higher learning and may even turn into dead weight. Time and time again the college-minded student inadvertently seeks familiarity or stays in the comfort zone of long-standing relationships. Be watchful of always taking the low fruit or keeping connections to mediocre people, especially while in the season of striving for more. At first glance, these people are coined as harmless, as they do not squander much of our time. But upon taking a closer look, we see these interactions tend to leave us unfulfilled.

Neutral energy is derived from people who sort of hang around aimlessly. From our perspective, we reason, "…they have always been my friend," while from the other person's perspective, they see interaction with a person like us as a badge of honor. What is daunting about this neutral energy is that they do not push our endeavors along, as they usually have no endeavors of their own. They harbor the "why rock the boat" mentality. Their mindset, coupled with a mediocre outlook on life, leaves them stuck. Without ill will, they question our ambitions with a "who does she think she is" mindset.

To illustrate, let's consider the lay of the land and scenario between two close friends Jillian and Carla:

Lay of the Land: Jillian and Carla have a well established relationship of seven years. They have kept a strong bond two years past high school. Jillian decided to bypass higher learning to pursue and land a nice-paying job while Carla stayed focused on her dream of going to college. She attends a local community college close to home.

Scenario: *Jillian: Are you available Friday night? I got us some tickets to that concert we were talking about. Do not stand me up this time.*

Carla: Hmmm…it's tempting but I have to pass…I have that take-home exam due by next Tuesday. If I do well I can bring my C up to an A.

Jillian: Awww, come on…Tuesday is forever away. Besides it's a take-home exam, right? You can do it anytime. Right?

Carla: (laughing) Jill, I don't know. Let me think about it.

Jillian: You have changed, these days you are always putting school over our friendship.

What can we get from this scenario? Holding a space for people such as Jillian provides Carla with a false sense of overachieving. Especially when Jillian has said such things in the past as, "Be easy on yourself, you have already made it," or "Live a little." In reality we need people that help us realize, or at least support, our goals. Be cautious as the "…they have always been my friend" notion can turn into the "I don't want to outgrow my friends" mindset, chipping away at our ambitions.

To summarize our discussion about the dead weight of neutral energy let us consider a basic scenario:

Think of a 4-person rowboat navigated by a lone rower to transport a fully occupied craft to the other side of a pond. In other words, one rower is doing the work of transporting himself and three other people across the body of water while the other three passengers enjoy the ride. Consider the dead weight of all the passengers being supported by the lone rower over the long haul. Over time the lone rower could come to resent the lack of help from the other passengers.

With the help of just one of the passengers, the journey would be much easier and completed faster. Think of the energy that can be ignited with assistance coming from all of the passengers. This level of cooperation would make the voyage easier and a situation *where everyone would win.*

We must be vigilant of not allowing too much neutral energy within our environment, as neutral energy is simply dead weight which many times turns into negative energy.

Negative Energy

Negative energy is much more pronounced than neutral energy—and once positive energy now drains us. In some cases, it can make us physically sick even in anticipation of being within the vicinity of certain people and environments. No matter how mentally prepared we try to make ourselves, we become defenseless. We tend to reason that the situation or person we are around is temporary. But even after a brief interaction has ended, we find ourselves emotionally exhausted. Regardless of our best efforts, especially in higher learning, each and every time we are in such situations, our peace of mind is compromised. For the college-minded student such energy is counterproductive, as it squanders our mental energy.

To illustrate, consider the lay of the land and a scenario from my personal catalogue of life:

Lay of the Land: I had a long-standing friendship with a person whom for this scenario I will call Jane. All and all, Jane was a good friend. We were each other's confidants in many matters of the heart. No relationship-based topic was off limits for a discussion. Through the years we cried and laughed together. The magic of our friendship was that we primarily texted/emailed and occasionally had phone conversations. On rare occasions, I would visit her in her hometown.

Scenario: *One of those rare occasions, our friendship took a turn for the worst. During a visit I made the mistake of starting a long-distance relationship with her good friend. In the midst of the courtship, I recall the day Jane and I made a pact. If my relationship hit the fan and did not work out, Jane and I would maintain our tight-knit bond. As it turned out, things did not work with the individual.*

The breakup was emotionally overwhelming and it affected almost every area of my life. Through it all I resolved to keep Jane away from the once flying sparks (between the ex and I) to retain our bond. She sincerely tried to play her normal position as my confidant, which at this time did not feel comfortable since she and my ex were friends. The ex would come up in conversations but over time I tried to refrain from those discussions as I was trying to heal. It felt emotionally unhealthy so I decided not to talk about my ex.

At one point, Jane questioned the emotional distance and my energy. I told her that I was still healing and to give me time. She wanted to continue to communicate, expecting the same level of intimate conversations. I knew subjecting myself to reopening wounds that were healing was unhealthy. Disheartened, I tried to honor our pact of staying close. Then one day during text communication where she was not getting the level of energy she was accustomed to, she abruptly said, "goodbye." Before honoring her request I asked her for further clarification with no communication in return until later the next year.

About eight months later, when she reached out I held her to her "goodbye."

What can we get from this scenario? First, let's be clear that we need people in our lives. People—good people—are not expendable. To go to the next level in higher learning we have to, on a case-by-case basis, distance ourselves from negative interactions. It is key to channel only healthy energy in times of stress. At the time, the relationship was not conducive to where I was going in my life. Remember that energy either grows or deteriorates. Both cannot occupy the same space. Mistakenly, we often hold the mindset that certain people are grandfathered into our lives. The life hack for negative energy is plain and simple: immediately develop an exit strategy.

Aside from negative energy there is another type of energy that must be recognized and has a category of its own—energy zappers.

Energy Zappers

Finally, energy zappers can be the most toxic to deal with—especially when we are pursuing higher learning. This is because we never know what to expect from these individuals. At times they consider themselves an integral part of our circle of support. While at other times the negative energy that lies dormant makes its grand entrance at the most inconvenient times. In almost all instances, the most toxic relationships we have are with people that we love and hold in high esteem, such as our parents, siblings, and/or spouse. In other instances, it could a pessimistic classmate we must deal with for a semester. Limiting interaction can be tricky based on the dynamics of the relationships and the level of mandated interactions.

Winners realize that the best life hack to deal with these energy zappers is to wish someone well but love from a distance. In this way, we are able to isolate ourselves from the negative vibes. Remember, from the first moments of our day we have a home-court advantage on how energy is channeled.

To again illustrate energy channeling, consider the relationship between family members Aunt Nancy and her niece, Allison. Nancy's adult-aged niece and others in the family have grown accustomed to her rants. Unknown to her, family members have coined her as Negative Nancy, knowing she has her good days and bad days. Imagine the level of pessimism she has caused amongst the family. Though now she is away at school most of the time, her niece Allison has grown tired of the negativity. Through years of experience with Aunt Nancy, Allison has found a way to distance herself from the pessimistic vibes and in this way offset the negative energy. Consider how Allison has perfected the energy channeling technique in this scenario:

Lay of the Land: Allison is on break from college and home for the annual family picnic. Having not been home for some time, Allison makes her rounds to each picnic table to greet everyone. As she approaches the picnic table where Aunt Nancy is seated, she makes several observations. Aunt Nancy's stern voice is overpowering the music, she is waving her hands to and fro, and everyone around Aunt Nancy has overwhelmed expressions on their faces. Based on the observations Allison thinks quickly on her feet. She assumes this is not a good day for Aunt Nancy, but instead of turning away she makes her approach to the table.

Scenario: *Allison: Good afternoon, everyone. Auntie, you are looking especially lovely. You wear red well. So nice to see everyone today!*

Aunt Nancy: Good afternoon, thank you.

What can we get from this scenario? Allison knows Aunt Nancy is an energy zapper. Allison saw the interaction as inevitable so she takes the initiative to spread positive energy. Without sacrificing a sincere greeting for Aunt Nancy, and protecting her own peace of mind, Allison used the life hack of energy channeling.

Remember all people have energy. Regardless of someone being a family member, a friend, or classmate, we have the right to be surrounded by healthy and fulfilling relationships. People within our circle of support who make contributions to their own lives are in a position to make a contribution to the lives of others. When thinking about relationships, think quality over quantity. It is OK to put boundaries around what kind of energy we deem as acceptable and unacceptable in our lives by repositioning the seating chart. Most college-minded students who are successful in higher learning do the work of seeking people who exhibit positivity and isolating themselves from people who exhibit negativity. Channeling energy works. The art of dominating the Winner's circle for the college-minded student means homing in on the most dynamic energy possible to not only win but gain traction for our "why".

The Winner's Creed

- Winners learn all people have energy.
- Winners learn there is no substitute for being around uplifting individuals who aspire to positively impact others and themselves.
- Winners learn to be vigilant of not allowing too much neutral energy within our environment, as neutral energy is simply dead weight.
- Winners learn it is OK to put boundaries around what kind of energy we deem as acceptable and unacceptable in our lives by repositioning the seating chart.

A person's energy can tell you more about them than their own word.

—Anonymous

LIFE HACKS FOR NURTURING THE BODY

Historically, students living on a college campus gain approximately ten pounds within their first year. This is because of a sedentary lifestyle and reliance on eating the overly processed, yet convenient foods available on the college campus. As we know, some foods can be enjoyed often (e.g., fruits, vegetables, and whole grains), while others should be enjoyed infrequently such as foods that are high in saturated fats, bad cholesterol (LDL), sodium/salt, and sugars (e.g., pizza, loaded potatoes, and baked goods).

The college campus cafeteria is notorious for those "eat infrequently" foods being offered daily and on demand! Though nicely stocked salad bars and fresh fruits are often available, many college students unfortunately do not take advantage of this rainbow of real foods. Many busy and overly hungry individuals would much rather go for a quick bite to eat. Far away from the watchful eye of Mom, there are food stations full of pasta, a host of creamy soups, buttered vegetables, marinated cuts of beef, fried foods, and pizza with toppings to accommodate everyone's taste buds. The buffet is a haven for grease, meat, and empty carbohydrates (e.g., starchy vegetables, hot rolls, a variety of rice and pasta). Of special interest are the stations well stocked with meals labeled, "made to order." Some students are misled when they see this, thinking these items are a reasonable stand-in for a home-cooked meal. Unfortunately, cheese seems be to be the running theme for all foods here, including cheesy omelets, grilled cheese sandwiches, and cheesesteak hoagies. To conclude meals, the college student is tempted with dessert. Warmed pastries, soft cookies, or a soft-serve ice cream cone have been some college students' favorites.

For many living on the college campus, exposure to the smorgasbord of foods is a new experience and takes on a life of its own and thus unwanted weight gain. Outside of the added pounds, an unhealthy diet is apparent through low energy and poor stress management.

Stress is unavoidable. In fact, stress can make us eat too much or too little. Some individuals do not understand that mental health is linked to a well-balanced diet. A life hack many college-minded students use is consuming foods rich in vitamins and minerals. These nutrient-packed foods help maintain health and the mental clarity needed to win in higher learning. Many students will attest they feel best when they limit portion sizes along with processed foods (overly sweetened and/or salted foods). Fresher foods with limited ingredients are instant sources of energy to promote mental clarity.

Superfoods

No diet is perfect, but part of dominating the Winner's circle means taking responsibility early in life to nurture our body, choice by choice. A poor diet is counterproductive to reaching our "why." What food people choose to eat is a personal choice that should be respected. Some people make the conscious choice to develop personal dietary goals and adapt to an eating regimen that works best for their lifestyle. This looks different for different people. For example, one person may simply want to limit portion sizes, while another person may choose to increase water consumption. Yet another person may decide to limit red meats. Though not a new practice, these days, people are reaping the benefits of superfoods. The beauty of these foods is they have a simple presence and are available almost everywhere, including on the college campus. Here is a list of some superfoods to consider:

- Spinach can be the base of a wholesome salad or steamed as a side. It is fully packed with disease-fighting nutrients including iron, fiber (which keeps us fuller longer), folic acid, lutein, calcium, magnesium, and vitamins A and K. Be sure to rinse it well before consuming. Not much of a spinach eater? Try stacking spinach high on a sandwich and/or a vegetable omelet.

- Oatmeal can be enjoyed any time of day and not just as a breakfast food. Most college campuses will have large containers of oatmeal available for those wanting a quick bite. A hot bowl of oatmeal that can be cooked in minutes is a complete meal coupled with such things as nuts, fruit, cinnamon, and honey. Oats have high levels of iron and fiber and the ability to reduce bad cholesterol.

- Salmon, known for its brilliant color and versatility, contains omega-3 fatty acids. This high-quality superfood has healing effects on inflammatory conditions and improves the circulation of blood flow throughout the body. Eating this healthy fish boosts brain function, especially important when mental agility is essential. Eating no more than two servings per week is generally fine, unless otherwise indicated.

- Tuna is another superfood. Just a small portion can contain only 70 calories but 15 grams of protein. Tuna is packed with many health benefits that include reducing the risk of a stroke and promoting heart and mental health. Specific nutrients include omega-3 fatty acids, iron, vitamin D, and of course protein. It's a great alternative to beef and pork without the excessive cholesterol.

- Walnuts, undeserving of their bad rap, boast healthier kinds of fats. Just a handful is rich in omega-3 fatty acids, iron, vitamin E, fiber, etc. If eaten in limited amounts, meaning just a handful daily, walnuts can fight cancer, delay disease states, and reduce LDL.

- Almonds are a great source of protein. Just one serving, about a handful, has approximately 13 grams of protein. Almonds are also rich in B vitamins, fiber, and calcium. Slivered pieces of almonds can complement both a fruit and vegetable salad. A small amount of almonds mixed with dry fruit can be a quick and healthy snack.

♟ Apples commonly eaten are Gala, Red Delicious, Granny Smith, and Fuji. There are over seven thousand different kinds of apples, with many grown in the state of Washington. As a simple carbohydrate, it breaks down quickly to give us immediate fuel. An apple eaten in its natural form is rich in fiber, has the ability to regulate blood sugar levels, and is high in antioxidants. Like almonds, apples can complement both a fruit and vegetable salad.

As mentioned earlier, the college campus cafeteria has some good options. Coupled with the desire to make a few healthy choices, high-quality foods can be found in the college campus cafeteria. We should not be overburdened with trying to have perfect eating habits. Rather consider balance and consistency while making high-quality choices (e.g., water instead of soda) a priority. When trying to eat healthier, the small steps truly matter.

Not seeing the high-quality foods you like and need in the college campus? Just ask! The college-minded student who dominates the Winner's circle will tactfully inquire about foods that may not be readily available or comparable options. The squeaky wheel gets the oil. In other words, most often when the dietary suggestions students make are collective, the campus decision-makers will take note and, over time, action. Using the life hack of ensuring that we are nurturing our bodies is a health habit worth exploring and mastering. It's the gift we can give ourselves and those around us, daily, over time, and well beyond college.

The Winner's Creed

♟ Winners learn stress is unavoidable.

♟ Winners learn fresher foods with limited ingredients are instant sources of energy to promote mental clarity.

♟ Winners learn that these days, people are reaping the benefits of superfoods.

♟ Winners learn that high-quality foods can be found in the college campus cafeteria.

You are what you eat.

—Unknown

41

LIFE HACKS AND SCENARIOS

The next section of this book will focus on introducing a plethora of life hacks and scenarios. You will notice each section is based on educational level, which will assist in sharpening interpersonal skills wherever you are in your journey. You are challenged with collecting information about the lay of the land and helping the student in each scenario find a solution for their problem. As an option, use the remainder of the space provided to add notes and reflect. After working through each scenario, use the suggestion-key planted in the back of the book to gain more insight (see Appendix D).

Consider this book as a reference which you refer back to often as you climb the academic ladder.

It's possible.

—Les Brown

High School

Life Hack #1: Use the Air Mask

We have all taken a flight and heard the flight attendant give instructions on how to keep safe in the rare case of an emergency. In particular, they demonstrate the procedure for using an air mask, should it deploy. Their instructions urge passengers to secure their own air mask first before helping others. Daily we have opportunities to use our air mask first.

Scenario: Carla, a high school senior, has a long-standing friend whose grandparent passed away two months ago. Her friend is taking the death hard and it is affecting every facet of her life. She confided in Carla that she may have to drop out of college for a semester to deal with her emotions. At this point, she has started to call Carla late at night to talk. She is always very grateful for Carla's listening ear yet it is taking a toll on Carla's sleep and productivity in classes the following day. Outline 2 or more ways Carla can help her friend in her time of need while keeping a handle on her own life.

_____

_____

_____

_____

_____

_____

_____

_____

_____

_____

_____

_____

_____

_____

Life Hack #2: Accept the Apology

When someone wrongs us, a simple apology could have the ability to mend hard feelings. The reality is sometimes we will never get the apology from a wrongdoer that we deserve, for a variety of reasons. Harboring feelings of resentment over time only hurts us. Quietly forgiving an offender does not let the offender off the hook. The offender will always have to live with their unsettled infraction, while we move forward with our lives. Accept the apology you never receive.

Scenario: David (a high school junior) and his girlfriend of over a year decided to part ways amicably. He learned an acquaintance of his from class, Ron, has started to date her and, in fact, she cheated with him during their courtship. David was upset. After all, he initially introduced them to each other. He has been ridiculed for retaining a friendly demeanor with them both. A month later, they break up. These days, when he sees his ex-girlfriend's ex-lover, David notices him lowering his head in shame. Today David learned he will be taking a class with Ron this coming school year. Outline 2 or more ways David can make peace with Ron and move forward.

_____

_____

_____

_____

_____

_____

_____

_____

_____

_____

_____

_____

_____

Life Hack #3: Own the Room

The moment people meet us, they start to develop a perception of who we are. This is a natural occurrence. In seconds, we are judged based on what others see and hear. It is unnerving but we have an opportunity to orchestrate our grand entrance on most occasions. Making eye contact as appropriate, wearing suitable attire, and speaking with confidence allow us to own the room.

Scenario: Kellie, a high school senior, has applied for a small humanitarian-based scholarship. Through a letter, she learned that she is a finalist. The scholarship committee has scheduled her for a time next week for a panel interview. Kellie's teachers and friends are excited for her, but she wonders if she can pull off the interview successfully. Name 2 or more ways Kellie can boost her confidence before the interview.

_____

_____

_____

_____

_____

_____

_____

_____

_____

_____

_____

_____

_____

_____

_____

Life Hack #4: Room for Calm

Make no mistake about it, being a student has its challenges. Juggling competing priorities can be overpowering. Moments of stillness are sometimes needed to regain perspective. These are the times we need to collect our thoughts to harness mental clarity. Giving ourselves a time-out allows room for calm.

Scenario: Academically, Derek, a high school senior, has been doing very well. Because of all his hard work, he landed an acceptance letter to a highly rated college out of state. If he is able to maintain this momentum, he will graduate from high school at the top of his senior class. However, he is worn out and just wants to throw in the towel. It seems like the more he gives, the more people expect. Come up with 2 or more ways to prevent Derek from burning out.

_____

_____

_____

_____

_____

_____

_____

_____

_____

_____

_____

_____

_____

_____

_____

Life Hack #5: Have a Happy Zone

Stress is here to stay, it is a regular part of life. All stress is not equal. Life presents less than optimal circumstances on a regular basis. There are some circumstances we cannot change, therefore we must adjust our mindset. In the meantime, why not choose to embrace the slightest moments of happiness? Purposely find things that bring contentment. Consider the joy of a smile, petting a dog's fur, or even indulging in a cup of hot coffee. Find ways to get into the happy zone, even for brief moments.

Scenario: Brian, a high school junior, wakes up feeling much better as he is just getting over a weeklong nasty cold. Today has been designated for studying for a test tomorrow morning. With Brian's newfound strength to study, he decides to turn off his cell phone. But before he does, he notices an incoming call from his boss, Joanna. Today, she needs him to complete a 6-hour shift at the coffee shop and states he is her last resort. Brian has a great relationship with his boss and can use the extra money, so he agrees. As Brian hangs up, anxiety starts to take over. Outline 2 or more ways Brian can maintain a peaceful day.

_____

_____

_____

_____

_____

_____

_____

_____

_____

_____

_____

_____

_____

Life Hack #6: Clean Eater

Though it is not a new phenomenon, these days there is much more conversation about clean eating and what it entails. In a nutshell, clean eating means consuming foods in their most natural form and finding ways to eliminate processed foods. For some people, determining to eat clean or transforming into being a clean eater is a process. Actively seek others who embrace those habits we want to obtain. Committing to finding ways to be a clean eater is a fight worth winning.

Scenario: Omar, a high school junior, learns yet another person in his family has developed type 2 diabetes. He is thinking about some of the unhealthy foods he eats in the high school cafeteria. Saddened, he resolves to change some eating habits. When he informally hints to friends that he wants to eat better, they tell him he is too young to worry. In other words, they do not appear to be supportive. Outline 2 or more ways Omar can clean up his diet and eat healthier even away from home.

_____

_____

_____

_____

_____

_____

_____

_____

_____

_____

_____

_____

_____

_____

Life Hack #7: Deliberate Action

Goals require precise energy. Some goals are accomplished while others remain a thought. Each one of us has an opportunity to make an impact. Nothing worth having comes easily. Making the best decisions are sometimes hard. Through the growing pains we must immerse ourselves in our vision. Without deliberate action, our heart's desire will remain a thought.

Scenario: Eldra is a high school senior scholar and has been feeling out of the loop by association with her seemingly nerdy friends. She yearns to build friendships with some of the 'cool' kids. Lately she has been asked to sit at the cool table by a popular classmate. Eldra is starting to embrace the newfound attention from the cool students. Today she received a secret invite to attend a cut party (bypassing school for the day to hang at someone's house). She knows illegal drug usage, sex, and drinking goes on at these parties. In her mind, she thinks attending one time should not hurt. On the day of the party, there is a big test for which she has been studying hard. Outline 2 or more ways Eldra can keep things in perspective.

_____

_____

_____

_____

_____

_____

_____

_____

_____

_____

_____

_____

_____

Life Hack #8: Assigned Seating

To keep order in a theater, seats are assigned. Assigning seats to the people in our lives has the ability to serve the same purpose. It keeps order. Think of how much time we allot to certain people in our lives. Perhaps our children receive more time while friends may receive much less time. Similar to arranging our schedule and priorities, we are able to rearrange the seats in the orchestra, mezzanine, and balcony of our circle of support. Be unapologetic—assign the seats in your life wisely.

Scenario: Melody, a senior in high school, received notice that she may be eligible for a scholarship that will help with tuition to the college of her choice. Consideration is contingent on graduating from high school with a higher GPA than she has now. She is determined to kick it up a notch by associating with more like-minded students. Melody reasons this will certainly increase her GPA. Outline 2 or more ways Melody can learn how to position herself around like-minded people.

_____

_____

_____

_____

_____

_____

_____

_____

_____

_____

_____

_____

_____

_____

Life Hack #9: Earn the Comfort

With conveniences of life on demand, we almost want for nothing. With technology everywhere people expect everything to happen faster. Without discipline, we rob ourselves of deserving the small prizes in life and developing a true reward system. Pay the dues and earn the comfort.

Scenario: Ken, a high school senior, has had a job for the last two years. With the money, he plans to save enough for a new computer, as he will be entering college soon. To his surprise, the new boss is giving everyone a holiday bonus. The extra money will equate to a month's pay. Ken is overwhelmed with this news and is starting to think about other big-ticket items he may need for his first year in college. Outline 2 or more ways Ken can use the bonus money for other expenses in college.

Life Hack #10: Come Out Swinging

Life has a way of knocking us down. When it comes to obtaining a measure of success, no one will grab our hand and guide us to our goals. Life does not work that way. Most goals that are accomplished happen through a vision. Make the choice to conquer life challenges, then come out swinging.

Scenario: Pricilla, a high school junior wants to go to college however she has a low GPA. At one time, she was making good grades but (self-admittedly) started running with the wrong group of friends in her sophomore year of high school. Thereafter, her grades faltered. Pricilla has resolved to bring her GPA back up, as she wants to gain acceptance into a local community college. She does not know where to start. Describe 2 or more ways Pricilla can get her grades back on track.

Life Hack #11: Hold the Vision

As we look ahead, sometimes our vision is clouded. In these instances, we must have the foresight to channel into our inter-being and literally pull out the person we could be. In this way we can see ourselves already accomplished. Whatever the feat, it starts with holding the vision.

Scenario: Tory has a goal of completing a marathon before graduating from high school. This is only natural as she has been on several sports teams over the years. Tory learns she has a friend who has completed three marathons and he has agreed to help her train. He is a little over the top with the early morning runs and motivational tactics but she keeps reasoning to herself that he knows what he is doing. Develop 2 or more ways Tory can stay focused on completing her goal.

_____

_____

_____

_____

_____

_____

_____

_____

_____

_____

_____

_____

_____

_____

Life Hack #12: Live a Simple Life

Commercials we see on television or billboard advertisements for material items can be overwhelming. We seem to always be willing to buy. It is easy to get wrapped up in a constant cycle of acquiring new things. These things we want are usually just that—wants. What would happen if we deaden our desire for new possessions and direct our attention and care on the things we already possess? Live simply, make the old new again.

Scenario: Anderson, a high school junior, is proud of himself. He has been doing a good job of saving money to attend a weeklong college fair road trip. This bus trip will go across four states in five days visiting fifteen colleges. As a junior in high school, this will be his first time out of the state, let alone away from home. Anderson dreams of one day attending college away from home. During a meeting about the pending trip, he overhears people talking about all the extras they will need to ensure they are comfortable on the bus. With just having enough to cover the cost of the trip, he starts to feel inadequate. Think of 2 or more ways Anderson can keep his mindset on track.

_____

_____

_____

_____

_____

_____

_____

_____

_____

_____

_____

_____

Life Hack #13: Smell Life

When was the last time we had an opportunity to appreciate all of our five senses (sight, touch, taste, hearing, and smell)? For example, think of our ability to smell. We can readily use our sense of smell to detect unpleasant or alarming odors. To be intentional about breathing and appreciating fresh air is rare. Live life passionately, determine to smell everything life has to offer.

Scenario: Within the last month Carson, a high school senior, did not have the opportunity to exercise. Carson comes from a family that values physical activity. He is thinking of freshening up his physical activity regimen to get back on track. Carson's friends invite him to join them as a guest with a local nature-based hiking group. This would be new to him, but he is ready to explore nature. Outline 2 or more ways Carson can intentionally use any of his five senses (sight, smell, touch, hearing, and taste) to fully enjoy the group hike.

_____

_____

_____

_____

_____

_____

_____

_____

_____

_____

_____

_____

_____

_____

_____

College Freshman

Life Hack #14: Be a Conversationalist

Being able to hold a good conversation is an invaluable trait. The main way of staying in the conversation with another person is the ability to not talk but merely listen. It is a natural inclination to want to interrupt the one sharing by noting our own comparable experience. But we open the door for even more sharing from others when we replace the urge to interject with even more listening. Embrace the joys of being a good conversationalist by attentively listening.

Scenario: Harley, a college freshman is nervous about her first day of school. In fact, at this moment, she is sitting in her first college class. As she looks around she notices that she is sitting in a classroom full of upper classmen that she has seen around the campus. Harley nervously sits at her desk when someone whom she recognizes from her dorm comes and sits beside her. Outline 2 or more ways Harley can use conversationalist skills in this situation.

_____

_____

_____

_____

_____

_____

_____

_____

_____

_____

_____

_____

_____

Life Hack #15: Be Amazed

Being around familiar surroundings and people brings a level of comfort. Like an old pair of shoes, we know each curvature, and comfort is assured each time. But what if we step out of our cozy shoes and into something brand new? What is the worst that can happen, besides a new experience? In the same way, try to embrace new people, experiences, and places daily. Seek ways to be amazed.

Scenario: Joslyn, a college freshman, has always sung in the shower but never thought of singing in front of others. She and a few new friends have started to frequent a small karaoke establishment in town. Tonight they challenge her to come back the next week prepared to sing a country song. Not only does she not sing in front of others, but she knows nothing about country music. Name 2 or more ways Joslyn can wrap her mind around the challenge.

_____

_____

_____

_____

_____

_____

_____

_____

_____

_____

_____

_____

_____

_____

Life Hack #16: 'Tis the Season

During festive times of the year we tend to spend more time with loved ones and friends. Several of these events are focused around eating. Healthier dishes are slim to none on most menus. At these times, it is tempting to stray away from our healthy habits. But there is hope. While arranging outings to socialize, it is just as important to keep health at the forefront of the schedule. Consider gravitating to the people who exemplify healthier habits that align with our goals. 'Tis the season to socialize but health should always be on the menu.

Scenario: Winter has been a busy time for Angel, a college freshman. Outside of taking two classes during the winter session, she works and tries to go to the gym at least a few times per week. This weekend, Angel has been invited to a holiday party where her boyfriend wants to introduce her to his family and closest friends. Her plate is full with needing to complete a take-home exam and work her part-time job. Outline at least 2 ways Angel can schedule being healthy this weekend.

_____

_____

_____

_____

_____

_____

_____

_____

_____

_____

_____

_____

_____

Life Hack #17: Warm Greetings Matter

The first moments of a conversation with a new person sets the tone for all future interactions. Consider a greeting. The first words can set the stage for the flow and even the duration of the conversation. Think of the last time someone took the leap and introduced themselves to you. Potentially, it left you vulnerable to reciprocate in the same exact manner. The next time a seemingly difficult conversation is on the line, try to remember that warm greetings matter.

Scenario: Jessica, a college freshman, has always been considered an introvert amongst her family and friends. In fact she was voted quietest in her senior class of high school. Most times, her greetings do not sound like much more than a whisper. Now that she is in college she has hopes of being involved in clubs and writing for the college newspaper. She wants to become more vocal and make connections. Outline 2 or more places Jessica can go to interact with others.

Life Hack #18: Laugh at Yourself

We live in an era in which we are groomed to be perfectionists with limited room for errors. This is especially true in the professional world. Real life does not always happen that way. The reality is we all make blunders. Some mistakes we can readily laugh at ourselves soon after. Life is too short to be serious all the time. Let's be light on our feet, let's learn to laugh at ourselves.

Scenario: Ted, a college freshman, is taking a swimming class as an elective this semester. Late as usual, today Ted walks hurriedly into the wrong class (a female-only class, in fact!) He is shirtless and in his swim trunks. They start to laugh and he runs out, dresses, and leaves. Later that day one of the young ladies (whom Ted has never met before) recognizes him from his blunder and approaches him at the local arcade. Laughing, she relives the mistake from that morning. Outline 2 or more ways Ted can brush off the incident while staying friendly.

Life Hack #19: Fulfill a Duty

Some people have dedicated their lives in service to others or have developed ideas that have benefited all mankind. Our time on earth is our time. However, it is always important to make a mark by giving back. Just think about the planes we see daily flying high in the skies. Large jets were made to accommodate hundreds of passengers. What if the Wright brothers' creation of the airplane was for self and never expanded to include planes beyond one seat? Freedom to travel would be limited. We all have an obligation to fulfill a duty and make an impact.

Scenario: Heaven is now a college freshman. She has retained a great relationship with her high school counselor. This same counselor helped her get into the college of her choice. Months ago the counselor reached out about a mentorship program she was developing for college hopefuls who were like Heaven. Heaven promised to help. The mentorship program will start soon and the counselor has checked in with Heaven to ensure she will donate her time as previously promised. Now Heaven's circumstances have changed. She is thinking of reconsidering. Outline 2 or more reasons Heaven has for honoring the commitment.

Life Hack #20: Build a Name

Think of some brand-name items you typically use and trust. It could be a certain brand of clothing or a household item. These days, our name is the calling card that speaks to our reputation—who we are and what we stand for. It's important to etch a calling card worth sharing. Be consistent about promoting your strongest attributes, and build a name.

Scenario: Kevin, a college freshman, is enrolled in an introductory college course that highlights use of self-efficacy skills. As part of a project, he is coupled with a partner to present a mock interview skit in front of the class. His partner is the interviewer hiring for a customer-service-based job, while Kevin will be the interviewee trying to obtain a job. He will need to come up with ways to sell himself and display workplace attributes in the skit. Outline 2 or more strong points Kevin could present during the skit.

_____

_____

_____

_____

_____

_____

_____

_____

_____

_____

_____

_____

_____

_____

Life Hack #21: Use Tact

Kind words can be used to defuse a strained interaction, repair a relationship, or soften the delivery of devastating news. There is weight in our words. It is often seen as a sign of weakness to speak softly and quietly. However, the person who is able to use tact (as needed) along with their choice of words has the ability to be more fully received.

Scenario: Otis, a college freshman, and his best friend attend the same out-of-state college, are from the same hometown, and have close family ties. Otis's friend's father calls him and tells him he is unable to reach his son. He asks Otis to deliver devastating news regarding his sister's car accident. She was seriously injured and his friend's dad asks Otis to bring him back home. Otis agrees. Outline 2 or more ways Otis can deliver the news to his friend.

_____

_____

_____

_____

_____

_____

_____

_____

_____

_____

_____

_____

_____

_____

_____

Life Hack #22: Catnap

Research states that sleep is required to revitalize the mind and body. In fact, specific bodily functions and repairs do not occur without the proper amount of sleep. Moments of rest can be sought any time of the day. Many people underestimate the value of small doses of sleep to calm a racing mind and bring clarity during peak hours of the day. The next time you feel drained, consider the joys of a catnap.

Scenario: Outside of being a freshman in college, Ivy started a part-time job working three evenings a week. Though she is taking 15 credits, she reasons this is what she needs to do to save for her upcoming spring break vacation in sunny Florida. The job starts an hour after her last class for the day and is a short walk from her dormitory. Outline 2 or more ways Ivy can find the time to rest before going to her job.

_____

_____

_____

_____

_____

_____

_____

_____

_____

_____

_____

_____

_____

_____

_____

Life Hack #23: Handwritten Note

Long gone is the use of the telegraph. Today we are afforded the opportunity to expedite communication at our fingertips. Most will agree that these manufactured modes of communication have smothered the ability to give a personal touch. Let someone special know you care. Let your thoughts flow by sending a handwritten note.

Scenario: Charles is a freshman in college. Coming from where he does, he never thought he would be on a college campus. Outside of his family, he has had some mentors from the community and his high school who have helped him gain acceptance into college. Charles wants to show his gratitude to these special people. Outline 2 or more ways Charles can show his gratitude for the people who helped him.

_____

_____

_____

_____

_____

_____

_____

_____

_____

_____

_____

_____

_____

_____

_____

_____

Life Hack #24: Etch it in Stone

It helps to visualize any goal. The bigger the goal, the more we must hold on tight. When the path to our goal gets tough, and it will, knowing our destiny brings a quiet calm. Many times people put their vision on paper. Etch it in stone, then live it.

Scenario: AJ, a college freshman, is on the brink of failing a biology class. His test grades have been low and attendance has been poor. He requests a time to meet with his professor to see what he can do to improve his grade. The professor doubts AJ will be able to pass but agrees to meet. As a condition he requests that AJ bring in his plan of action for dedicating more time to biology. Outline 2 or more ways AJ can present a solid plan.

_____

_____

_____

_____

_____

_____

_____

_____

_____

_____

_____

_____

_____

_____

_____

Life Hack #25: Clear the Air

At one point or another we have been offended and/or have offended someone else. Sometimes we do not find out about the infraction we inflict until much later. In other instances, there may be a semi-broken bond with a long-standing friend or family member that has been on shaky ground. It is the unspoken words that continue to cut the heart until a sincere apology is either said or received. By opening up the lines of communication and taking at least partial ownership of the infraction, we are able to move forward in peace. Kill the ego, then clear the air.

Scenario: Michelle is a new college freshman. Her best friend of several years has fully entered the workforce. Michelle realizes their friendship has changed. Her friend starts to break commitments to Michelle and even stand her up. Hurt by her friend's actions, she continues to operate in the same circle of friends but decides to keep her distance by not calling, returning communications the next day, and not asking to hang out. After a few months, via a text, her friend questions her actions. Consider 2 or more ways Michelle can start to clear the air.

_____

_____

_____

_____

_____

_____

_____

_____

_____

_____

_____

_____

Life Hack #26: Cultivate Inner Peace

Life truly has its ups and downs. Everything could be going seemingly perfect, then our life can come apart at the seams at any moment. During times of calm it may help to plan healthy escapes for the times when life's scenarios become overwhelming. Proper planning helps us steer clear of poor choices. It could be listening to a soothing tune, sitting quietly, or talking to a friend. Find ways to cultivate inner peace.

Scenario: Morgan, a college freshman, has always found joy in playing in the high school band but college is much different. She is in college on a scholarship for playing the trumpet. Meeting bandmates with high-level skills is rewarding but having to deal with new personalities is a challenge within itself. Name 2 or more ways Morgan can stay focused on her craft while learning how to work with new bandmates.

Life Hack #27: Say a Name

Each of our names holds uniqueness. We carry it with pride as we introduce ourselves to new people. We are especially impressed when a casual acquaintance remembers our name. Let's try to task ourselves with remembering a name. Practice makes perfect. Recalling a name and pronouncing it correctly gives a person instant gratification, even if not expressed aloud. Say a name.

Scenario: Erin, a college freshman, has always had issues with remembering names. This term she has a professor who has a name that is difficult to pronounce. Like her counterparts, Erin addresses him as "Professor" or "Sir." He seems to be content with this title, but she wants to address him by his proper name. Also, Erin foresees having a substantial amount of interaction with him for the next few semesters. Develop 2 or more ways Erin can address this issue and address the professor by his name.

_____

_____

_____

_____

_____

_____

_____

_____

_____

_____

_____

_____

_____

Life Hack #28: Something Unique

Wanting to be liked is healthy. But issues can creep in when the feeling we have for ourselves is contingent on how others feel about us. This can build a foundation of low self-worth leaving us in a constant cycle of looking for evidence of value from others to validate our worthiness. If we live a life of seeking signals of self-worth we deprive ourselves of the opportunity to truly accept ourselves. We all have something unique to offer the world, but it starts with offering it to ourselves.

Scenario: Annabella, a college freshman, has been feeling particularly lonely lately when she notices she has not been getting much communication (via phone) from friends or family back home. The text messages and evening calls from her college friends have died down, too. It seems like everyone is busy with school, new relationships, and/or seasonal jobs. She wonders if there is something wrong with her since people have turned cold suddenly. Come up with 2 or more ways that will help Annabella change her mood.

_____

_____

_____

_____

_____

_____

_____

_____

_____

_____

_____

_____

_____

_____

Life Hack 29: Seek Positive People

It is not too often that individuals accomplish things alone. An encouraging conversation from a supportive friend or loved one can be just what we need to push us along during a difficult time. Try to seek positive connections with others in even the briefest capacities. This could be through sharing a smile with fellow students and/or others. Let us sweeten our lives by seeking positive people.

Scenario: As an only child, Jasmine, a college freshman, has been a loner all her life. Previously, her time had been filled with a host of cousins who were always around, so she has always been content. Now that she is far away from home and in college, things are a little different. Jasmine wants to start to develop relationships but it's a challenge. Develop 2 or more plans of action that will help Jasmine connect with people.

_____

_____

_____

_____

_____

_____

_____

_____

_____

_____

_____

_____

_____

_____

Life Hack #30: Reclaim Your Time

The presence of social media has slowly seeped into everyone's life. The good news is that these platforms allow us to share pictures, memories, and even our feelings with the entire world. It's tempting to tune in for just a few moments to get updates. The bad news is that these veins of social media routinely deplete valuable moments, minutes, and hours out of millions of people's day with a scroll of a finger. We live in a society where getting updates has turned into an addiction. Reclaim your time, learn how to disconnect.

Scenario: Jewels, a college freshman, is taking a course that covers time-management basics. An assignment instructs her to keep a log of how she is spending blocks of time in 30-minute increments for three days. The goal is to learn which activities take up her time most often. At the end of the assignment, she tallies up her time to highlight the top three activities outside of class time. To Jewels's dismay, she learned seven hours were spent on social media sites. List 2 or more ways Jewels can decrease her time on social media.

College Sophomore

Life Hack #31: Superfoods

Over time, poor-quality foods with no real health benefits can affect our overall health. On the other hand, quality-rich foods are a necessity to keep us alive and well. The term superfood is a newer term coined for foods with high-quality nutrients that help our bodies perform at high levels of efficiency. Superfoods have the ability to heal and potentially ward off illnesses. To achieve higher levels of health, let us eat our superfoods daily.

Scenario: It has been a great semester for Steve. He and a few friends plan to commemorate the end of their sophomore year with a 4-day road trip covering several states in a few days. Amongst the bunch, Steve is the healthiest eater. Secretly he is concerned about his eating out on the open road, as he will not have access to his normal eating regimen. Outline at least 2 ways Steve can eat well even on the road.

Life Hack #32: The Art of Saying "No"

Have you ever heard the saying, if you want something done, give it to a busy person? It's true. Busy people seem to be more agreeable to putting more on their plates to help others. To a degree, this is OK. But constant requests or requests that infringe on your time can be overwhelming. Learning to draw the line in the sand may be hard but it helps us manage our time. To set boundaries, start with the art of saying "no."

Scenario: Douglas, a college sophomore, has worked six straight days preparing for an end of the semester presentation with his fellow classmates. Today, a relaxing day alone is planned. As he sits drinking his morning coffee and planning his day, the phone rings. It is a friend who calls to ask Douglas to come and help him shop for a car. The friend had another friend who pulled out at the last minute. Outline 2 or more ways Douglas can stay on track with his day.

_____

_____

_____

_____

_____

_____

_____

_____

_____

_____

_____

_____

_____

_____

Life Hack #33: Start Small

Our thoughts are one of the most powerful tools we have. Through accomplishing bite-sized steps we are able to accomplish anything. Think of being determined to get an A in a particular class. It starts with having a grasp of class expectations through reviewing the syllabus. Thereafter, micro-goals must be set to accomplish the macro-goals. This may include joining a study group, positioning ourselves with others just as driven, and potentially obtaining guidance from a tutor. People often feel deflated because they do not consider the minor details. Be driven but learn the magic of starting small.

Scenario: Shaun, a college sophomore, meets with his college advisor to map out his class schedule for the next semester. The advisor suggests that Shaun take both a science and a math class in the same semester. To add more pressure, Shaun has a goal of starting to take five classes this semester. Instead of the usual four classes, in order to graduate from college earlier. He feels overwhelmed but up for the challenge. Think of 2 or more ways Shaun can prepare for success before the semester starts.

_____

_____

_____

_____

_____

_____

_____

_____

_____

_____

_____

_____

Life Hack #34: Rise Early

Many successful people benefit from developing an early morning regimen. This may look different for different people. Waking up at least two hours earlier allows for mental clarity to use the time as we please, including time to study, exercise, or simply meditate. Rising early sets us up for a day of major gains.

Scenario: Linda, a college sophomore, has never been a morning person. Fortunately, she always lands afternoon and evening classes, which has worked out perfectly. Next semester there is no way around being enrolled in a 6:30 a.m. class, three days per week. Anxiety is getting the best of her. The next semester starts in three weeks. Describe 2 or more ways Linda can set herself up for success now.

_____

_____

_____

_____

_____

_____

_____

_____

_____

_____

_____

_____

_____

_____

_____

_____

Life Hack #35: Just Smile

It's hard to read an expression on the face of a stranger or someone whom we do not know. A smile reciprocates a smile. They are universal. It sets the stage for positive energy to flow in almost any situation. Additionally, starting an interaction with a smile has the ability to soften the tone of any interaction. The ability to grin at ourselves in our private moments even has the ability to brighten our own day. Hands down, a smile wins.

Scenario: This semester Jesus, a college sophomore, is in the midst of taking a late class three times per week. After all, he is a night owl so this class works perfectly in his schedule. Jesus learned quickly that other students are low energy and do not share his enthusiasm. It is the second week of class and outside of the professor, he feels like he is in a room full of zombies. The environment is somber. Outline 2 or more ways Jesus can stay engaged in the class.

Life Hack #36: Gratitude

Being grateful for the small things in life makes our worries less important. When we compare our lives to others, what can we glean? Though we are all faced with issues, there are always other people with more pressing problems. Many times people have found solitude in meditation. It is true we must live in our own reality, but when we operate in a space of gratitude for the small things, life can be a little less overpowering.

Scenario: Recently, Gina, a college sophomore, has been diagnosed with an illness that she must deal with so she has had to take some time off from school. The bright side is that over time with self-care and medicine, she will make a full recovery. Nonetheless, she can't help but feel sorry for herself. Though other things in her life are going well, she can't help but wonder why this is happening to her. Come up with 2 or more things to immediately increase Gina's sense of gratitude.

_____

_____

_____

_____

_____

_____

_____

_____

_____

_____

_____

_____

_____

Life Hack #37: Develop Muscles

When we are in a season of learning a new skill or accomplishing a particular goal, we must resolve to become stronger. This means that we must figuratively develop the muscles that have been lying dormant. At first, developing these muscles will be uncomfortable or even painful, but over time our developing new muscles will serve us well.

Scenario: College sophomore, Brett, is a math major. He is part of a cohort of other students in a series of math courses. As a newcomer, he learns that these students have worked as a group before and each of them is on the Dean's List (something he is hoping to accomplish too). With the exception of one Sunday per month, he finds the cohort is committed to spending each Sunday together as a group to review work and complete assignments. In Brett's world, Sundays are made for worship and relaxation. Consider 2 or more ways Brett can align himself with the cohort but make worship part of his schedule.

_____

_____

_____

_____

_____

_____

_____

_____

_____

_____

_____

_____

_____

_____

Life Hack #38: Decompress

We all have the need to decompress at times outside of sleep. Taking a pause means different things to different people. Some people find relaxation through a quick brisk walk, while others find peace in listening to loud music. Regular self-care shows self-love. Let us be kind to ourselves and find ways to decompress.

Scenario: Marissa, a college sophomore, is considering quitting the soccer team. This is a far cry from when she started in high school. Initially she wanted to stay fit, make friends, and potentially obtain a scholarship from her budding skills. While her plan is working well, she is dealing with an overbearing coach. Lately before practice, Marissa has anxiety attacks. She is not alone in her thoughts, as others have confided about the same issue. Describe 2 or more ways Marissa can decompress for moments during practice.

_____

_____

_____

_____

_____

_____

_____

_____

_____

_____

_____

_____

_____

_____

_____

Life Hack #39: Believe in Your System

A belief system is based on individual truths. Everyone has a system of knowingness, whether tightly or loosely organized. These truths are built on exposure to an array of respective experiences. Though life is about exposing ourselves to experiences that challenge us to grow, never compromise our beliefs until we, ourselves, have the information to change our perception. Let us freely believe in our system.

Scenario: Jack, a college sophomore, was not raised in the church but has always been spiritual, knowing there was a higher being. Now that he is in college he wants to start exploring religion at the local churches in town. He commits to go to one new church a month. Jack starts to go to one in particular and the people seem to be very friendly. They encourage him to continue to attend but it feels like pressure. Jack does not feel comfortable with some of the teachings. Outline 2 or more ways Jack can handle the pressure at the new church.

Life Hack #40: Resiliency

Very few people are able to accept hardships without crumbling from defeat. In fact, we try to avoid change like the plague. With hesitation we go through the necessary steps to move forward. When enduring a hardship, embrace the change and push through, remembering this too shall pass. Endure the storms because in those moments we build resiliency.

Scenario: Xavier, a college sophomore, is usually a happy-go-lucky person. But lately he has been going through a difficult time and has been stressed out. All in one week his roommate-turned-best-friend dropped out of school, he learned his parents are divorcing (after 25 years of marriage), and because of his poor grades last term he is on academic probation. Even with only taking three classes, it is hard to concentrate. Xavier is ready to throw in the towel. Determine 2 or more strategies Xavier can use to make it through this difficult time.

College Junior

Life Hack #41: Listen to Hear

In the midst of a debate with others we tend to be ready to hurl comments back, even before we hear what others have fully expressed. Upon closer examination, it is our egos that can get the best of us. Egos drown out our sense of reason for demanding justice. A battle of the egos can leave everyone frustrated. Try charging down. Attentively listening allows us to see the entire picture. Take it all in—listen to hear.

Scenario: Lou, a college junior, is in a research cohort this semester. To his surprise, his professor assigned him as the group leader. Most of the students seem to be accountable for their share of the workload to complete small parts of a large project. However, there is one student who continues to not pull her weight. Her passiveness is apparent, and some people are getting frustrated with her lack of productivity. One evening, Lou sees her coming out of the gym as he is entering. This is his chance to make a connection. Describe 2 or more ways Lou can approach his fellow classmate and have an informal discussion about the issue.

Life Hack #42: Monday Motivation

Think about the expression, "Thank God it's Friday" (TGIF). It signifies the end of a grueling week and ushers in an opportunity to relax. Additionally, many people see Friday as the start of the weekend and often a reason to throw caution to the wind. Alternately, Monday is seen as the most dreaded day of the week. However, Monday is a crisp start of what could be an amazing week. Moving into greatness starts with Monday motivation.

Scenario: Mary, a college junior, has never been a fan of Mondays. She has just enjoyed a much-needed 3-day weekend with friends. It's Sunday evening and she starts to look ahead at the upcoming week. Outside of Mary's normally scheduled classes, she has two exams and works her part-time job each night this week. Define 2 or more ways Mary can start out her week on firm ground.

Life Hack #43: Take Less Space

Some people find acquiring material things almost therapeutic. Not everyone aspires to build their lives around things. In fact they make an effort to master the art of living with less. The minimalist lifestyle is gaining momentum. Outside of being able to exert gratitude, removing stuff breeds intangible wealth. Taking less space welcomes peace and mental agility.

Scenario: Andrew, a junior in college, took a personal finance class last year. He has started the habit of saving money. He now leads a minimalist lifestyle and it serves him well. He started to date an intelligent young lady and they are now in a relationship. As they prepare for their final year of college, they are thinking of a long-term relationship and possibly marriage. However Andrew's concern is she loves to shop and, in Andrew's mind, wastes money. Outline 2 or more ways Andrew can approach his girlfriend about his lifestyle values.

_____

_____

_____

_____

_____

_____

_____

_____

_____

_____

_____

_____

Life Hack #44: See the Lesson

We all have experiences in our lives that have been devastating. Without allowing healing to take place, we remain imprisoned. Should we make the choice to move on from the situation, we are not immune to encounter the same experience again. However, we can build a resistance to help us move into new situations with wisdom. When we feel wronged, consider chalking it up and see the lesson learned.

Scenario: Jeff, a college junior, is in the same situation—again. He is in a study group at a local coffee shop and the same classmates have left him with the tab to pay. Though it's not a large amount of money Jeff must shell out, this is the second time it has happened this month. Being a student, he does not have a budget for extra expenses. Outline 2 or more ways Jeff can ensure this does not become a repeat occurrence.

Life Hack #45: Expand Horizons

As human beings we tend to mirror those people around us. That is why it is key to choose our circle of influence wisely. It can be an uphill battle to see growth when we associate with people who do not grow. In fact, when growth is not the focal point, we inadvertently become content with being less than our personal best. Let us fill our life with people who force us to expand horizons.

Scenario: Reese, a college junior, has had a work-study job on campus for almost two years. He has a great relationship with his supervisor, who informs him there is a supervisory position across campus and he suggests that Reese consider the job. This works for him for several reasons, which includes more flexibility and an increase in his hourly pay. However Reese has reservations, as he will be supervising a small group of his fraternity brothers whom he considers to be friends. Reese has never supervised anyone, let alone friends. Describe 2 or more ways Reese can adjust his mindset and take on the new position.

Life Hack #46: Change the Music

The human mind can take us every single place imaginable. A passing thought can spark a chain reaction for a change to an entirely new thought process. What we allow to be filtered in our mind, into our very space, makes a difference. Just think, by using our minds, we can change a somber tempo into an upbeat rhythm on demand. The next time we get the nagging gut feeling to do so, (figuratively) change the music.

Scenario: Shante, a college junior, has learned a lot from a small group of friends she has been acquainted with since her freshman year at college. Though she once saw them as close friends, she has become disheartened by some of their pessimistic mindsets over the last few months. Shante's friends' negative mindset seems to be rubbing off on her. Define 2 or more reasons Shante should reevaluate her friendships.

Life Hack #47: Strength in Numbers

There are many goals which could be accomplished alone. However, consider an easier way when the opportunity arises. Sharing time and energy with people who have like minds for the sake of a positive outcome is of value to all those involved. Think of an assembly line. Each person has a specific job in the process with the ultimate goal of building a quality product. It would only take one person falling short on the job to lessen quality. Seek worthwhile alliances and see strength in numbers.

Scenario: Jason, a college junior, has been agonizing about taking public speaking but this semester it's unavoidable. He has always shrunk away from being the center of attention. Today is the first day of his public speaking class and he makes observations about the people sitting up front. They seem to be comfortable in the class. In fact, as the instructor asks for each person to provide a brief introduction they take delight in sharing. Jason learns the first speech is due next week. Outline 2 or more ways Jason can align himself with the seemingly comfortable students.

_____

_____

_____

_____

_____

_____

_____

_____

_____

_____

_____

_____

_____

Life Hack #48: Watch Your Dividends Grow

Being wise with our time can be a juggling act. We have all had a friend learn that we had seemingly idle time on our hands and innocently enough filled it with their agenda. Though helping others brings a sense of fulfillment, just think of the things we could have accomplished by utilizing our own time. We need to be more conscious of casual interruptions and ultimately the way we allot our time. When we spend our time more often than not on ourselves, we watch our dividends grow.

Scenario: Rachel, a college junior, has been feeling overwhelmed with classes so decides to seek the help of a counselor to sort things out. Her counselor commends her for making an effort to take care of herself better during this time of high stress. He asks Rachel to complete an exercise where she will need to do a 24-hour recall of how she spends her time, hour by hour. Upon sharing, he tells her that she is cramming too much into a single day. He gives Rachel a homework assignment for the next session that entails some consideration about how to make time for herself. Consider 2 or more ways that Rachel can make more time for self-care each day.

College Senior and Graduate School

Life Hack #49: Fuel Your Body

Because of wear and tear, an older vehicle can run below expectations. As it is puttering along, we may try to add a higher grade of fuel. Premium fuel has the ability to improve the car's performance. The same happens with our bodies. Without adding quality fuel, we are simply puttering along. To improve our performance, choose premium fuel.

Scenario: Lately Don (a college senior) and his cohort of classmates are putting in several hours per week to complete a semester long project. After voting, a majority has chosen late-night hours (9:30 p.m. to 12:00 a.m.), three times per week. Staying up late like this and getting up for a 7 a.m. class is leaving Don exhausted. Come up with 2 or more ways to keep Don's momentum in the cohort while getting the rest he needs.

_____

_____

_____

_____

_____

_____

_____

_____

_____

_____

_____

_____

Life Hack #50: Your Possible

Many times we limit ourselves by not believing in our capabilities. Some of the goals we set seem so big that they scare us. When this is the case, we are on the right track. Be mindful that when we think small, we achieve small. Inadvertently, we gravitate to the safe zone where we grant ourselves an "off the hook" pass. We climb to higher heights when we believe in our possible.

Scenario: This semester Jacqueline, a college senior, is set to graduate from college but is at a crossroads. Her new goal is to continue her momentum in obtaining her terminal degree. But Jacqueline has gotten pushback from her family. They are pressuring her to move into the workforce and consider graduate school later. Jacqueline thrives off her family's approval. With no role models, she is starting to back away from her goal. Outline 2 or more ways Jacqueline can move forward in her decision to work on her advanced studies.

_____

_____

_____

_____

_____

_____

_____

_____

_____

_____

_____

_____

_____

_____

Life Hack #51: Informed Decisions

We make hundreds of decisions each day, from what shoes we will wear to how much time we will allot to sleep. So we are usually good at making quick, unimportant decisions. A majority of the decisions we make are not urgent. However, there are times when we are faced with having to make split-second decisions. When feasible, we must learn when to halt our decision-making process to collect our thoughts, gather more information, and make ourselves more knowledgeable. Being informed paves the way for making informed decisions.

Scenario: Chris, a college senior, is a proud member of a fraternity within his college. The pressure was high for him to be heavily involved in a community-based summer fundraiser, but he pulled through with flying colors. His fellow fraternity brother noted Chris's hard work and wants him to consider spearheading an upcoming citywide teenage male mentorship program. Outline 2 or more pieces of information Chris will need to make an informed decision.

_____

_____

_____

_____

_____

_____

_____

_____

_____

_____

_____

_____

Life Hack #52: Be Wrong

We are prone to be defensive when we know with all certainty we are correct. In the midst of a disagreement or debate think of this: how would it feel if we stopped sharing our facts and fully engaged ourselves in seeing things from another person's perspective? Of course this should not have to be done on each occasion, as we have the right to take up for ourselves. More times than not though, savor the weightlessness of being wrong.

Scenario: Ada, a senior in college, decides to officially take an introduction to writing class as an elective. Creative writing brings her peace and she wants to hone her skills. Ada already has a leg up on others, as she is familiar with the various writing styles. On the first day of class, she assumes everyone is new to creative writing. Ada quickly learns the instructor is new to instructing the course and seems a bit nervous. While checking behind the instructor using her assigned textbook, she notices the instructor herself may be learning some of the material on the fly. Outline 2 or more ways Ada can get the most out of the course while adjusting to a potentially new style of teaching.

_____

_____

_____

_____

_____

_____

_____

_____

_____

_____

_____

_____

Life Hack #53: Brick by Brick

We can't be wildly successful at everything we touch. However, there are things that can and will become our forte. Some people have a knack for the sciences or are savvy at mathematics. Other individuals have softer skills on the social side and are able to easily relate to others. Rather than focus on our weaknesses, why not concentrate on the things that make us extraordinary and build brick by brick.

Scenario: Augustine is a fashion major in her senior year of college. She has had an internship working with top designers where her work has been featured as a part of Fashion Week. Additionally, Augustine has built quite a reputation for her work around the college campus. A large-scale annual fundraiser is scheduled for three months away. School dignitaries will be in attendance. The college president's representative reaches out to her with a request. The president has an idea in mind and wants Augustine to design a dress using beads and pearls. She thinks this is out of her league, as she has never designed anything with such detail. The representative wants to meet with Augustine in two days. Outline 2 ways Augustine can build her confidence and take on the task.

_____

_____

_____

_____

_____

_____

_____

_____

_____

_____

_____

Life Hack #54: Stand on Shoulders

Based on our heritage and upbringing, we all have a unique background. In fact, those factors define who we are today. Though each of us is our own person and destined to create a unique legacy, we must know we come from people who wanted us to succeed. As we go about our lives and write our stories, it's imperative to know we stand on the shoulders of those before us.

Scenario: It has been ages since Marlene, a college senior, has seen her uncle who now lives out of town. He has always been one of her favorite people and were once very close. He is the reason she decided to go to college. Being in college, time has passed and Marlene has not communicated much throughout the last few years. He is planning to come to town this summer for the family reunion. Outline 2 or more ways Marlene can reconnect with her uncle while he is in town.

Life Hack #55: Be Choosy

Let us think about the people around us. Taking inventory of the people within our circle of influence speaks a lot about us. This is because upon closer consideration we will see that many times their aspirations are aligned with our exact goals. Therefore, it is fair to say we are as strong as our circle of influence. When we seek to go higher, we become keenly responsible for the company we keep. Reaching higher means we need to be choosy.

Scenario: Christina, a college senior, sincerely loves people. Over the last several years she has built relationships with people whom she considers true friends. Her friends enjoy the casual time spent together, especially on Friday nights and weekends. Now that Christina has become an upperclassman she is considering her next moves in life. She has thought about going to medical school. Her advisor (turned friend) suggests her 3.2 GPA may be a hindrance, recommends she bring up the GPA, and points out the need to put more time into her studies. Describe 2 or more ways Christina can create more time to study without putting too much of a strain on her social life.

_____

_____

_____

_____

_____

_____

_____

_____

_____

_____

_____

_____

Life Hack #56: Power of Touch

A tender touch at the right time can calm a fussy baby through reaffirming the maternal bond. The same gesture can help console a grieving heart. In almost all interactions with the people we care about, we are welcome to use hugs and rubs to provide comfort. A touch has the ability to soothe some pain and empowers others on their path to healing. With tact, use the power of a touch.

Scenario: Luz, a college senior, has decided to volunteer as a domestic abuse advocate for victims. This will work nicely as she plans to go into social work when she graduates. After a brief training tonight, she is on the job. For the very first assignment, Luz has been assigned to console a grieving student who is in her first semester of college. Allegedly the student's boyfriend assaulted her a few hours ago. Luz shows up to the designated dorm. Immediately anxiety fills her heart as she walks down the second-floor hall and stands at the student's dorm room. At this point she freezes. As she walks in, she sees the victim is her baby sister. Outline 2 or more ways Luz can make her sister feel comfortable.

Life Hack #57: New Genre

Music has the ability to reach into the farther parts of our souls. A catchy rhythm can make us want to sway from side to side and throw our cares to the wind. Before we know it, one song can lead into another song. We tend to gravitate to the music we were exposed to in our formative years or that evokes feel-good thoughts. Find the wonder in swaying to a different beat by exploring a new genre.

Scenario: Taylor, a college senior, has been raised in a household of jazz musicians. Sundays were made for the family to enjoy southern-style dinners along with her parents playing their favorite jazz songs. She was groomed to love jazz. Now that she is about to graduate from college, her family wants to host a large party equipped with a jazz band. Taylor has grown to equally love R&B, therefore she wants such music played. Outline 2 or more ways Taylor can compromise on the selection of music with her family for the graduation.

Life Hack #58: Be Joyous

Have you ever encountered a pessimist who, no matter what the circumstances, appears to only focus on the negative in life? Some even proclaim the entire day will be a bust because the weather is bad! With negative-minded people everything is to blame for the dissatisfaction within their lives. When we distance ourselves away from the negative, we allow space for light to shine. In spite of such people, be joyous.

Scenario: Lisa, a college senior, was delighted to have a new housemate this semester. However, she learned her new housemate has some traits that are disappointing. The housemate is overall a great person but Lisa learned quickly that she started her day with a negative disposition about her classes and life in general. Lisa likes to start her morning with meditating, as a way to calm anxiety. Amidst the negativity this has changed. After a month Lisa has learned that she is expected to serve as a sounding board. Outline 2 or more ways to take back her time and resume her morning routine.

Life Hack #59: Right a Wrong

We all try to be the best person we can be and do right by others. It's human nature to want people to feel comfortable in our presence. At some points, regardless of our best efforts, we may cause others discomfort or pain. Words spoken and even unspoken can put a strain on our relationships. When we learn to immediately remedy the matter at the root of the problem, we can save a fragile relationship and right a wrong.

Scenario: Dean, a college senior, was the star quarterback on his college football team a couple years ago. His football career ended when a teammate tripped him on the football field, causing him to injure his ankle beyond repair during the championship game. This incident caused Dean's team a major loss. He swore it was purposely orchestrated by this teammate. At the time, being in immense pain, Dean cursed him out in front of the entire football team. Recently after watching footage of the game, he saw he was wrong. Tomorrow they both will graduate. Define 2 or more ways Dean can right the wrong with his ex-teammate.

_____

_____

_____

_____

_____

_____

_____

_____

_____

_____

_____

_____

Life Hack #60: Walk Among the Runners

While we walk with another person, collectively a pace takes shape. If the other person increases their speed, we inadvertently increase our speed. If we were to merge into a fast-paced crowd, we step up our pace. Moving among people who have developed a calculated faster stride allows us to stretch ourselves. Walk among the runners.

Scenario: As a graduate student, evenings are Vivian's downtime. She takes pride in and enjoys getting a full night's sleep. Now that she has been accepted into the college's graduate program she is in a special dormitory. Vivian learns that students customarily work and have community-based commitments during the day. But it is the night hours that people use to delve deep into their studies. She learns about a particular group of scholars who meets at 10:30 p.m. on weeknights to help each other out with assignments and socialize. Vivian has been invited. Outline 2 or more ways Vivian can readjust her mindset and immerse herself into the nighttime routine.

APPENDIX A: WINNER'S CIRCLE MANIFESTO

Monday Manifesto

I Must	I Can	I Wish

Tuesday Manifesto

I Must	I Can	I Wish

Wednesday Manifesto

I Must	I Can	I Wish

Thursday Manifesto

I Must	I Can	I Wish

Friday Manifesto

I Must	I Can	I Wish

Saturday Manifesto

I Must	I Can	I Wish

Sunday Manifesto

I Must	I Can	I Wish

APPENDIX B: SCOTT'S ACTIVITY CHOICES—KEY

Roommate 1 Scenario: Scott is a college senior athlete and has many performance-based awards under his belt for football. He is the lead quarterback on the school's Division I football team. For him, Sundays were made for rest and relaxation. Today is Sunday, let's help Scott plan out his day. It may be useful to know Scott feels he has studied enough over the last several days—besides he reasons he needs only a C average to maintain his sports scholarship. In addition, he admits that outside of his friends on the football team, his relationships have suffered and he wants to strengthen personal bonds with others. How might Scott's Sunday manifesto look?

Exercise 2: Scott's Activity Choices

Choose Task	Activity	Rank Importance
X	Participate in a study group (1.5 hours)	3
	Revisit notes from the week's classes (1 hour)	
	Complete a cardiovascular workout (1 hour)	
X	Attend church (2 hours)	2
X	Grab brunch with a high school buddy (1.5 hours)	2
	Watch an animal-based documentary (3 hours)	
	Go grocery shopping (1 hour)	
X	Check in with parents (30 minutes)	1
	Register for fall classes online (15 minutes)	
	Do laundry (1.5 hours)	

Reasoning for Scott's Sunday Personal Manifesto:

Based on the information provided for this scenario, on weekdays Scott's focus is on being his best for his craft, which is football. Academically he feels as if he is doing what it takes to pass his courses. His concern is his lack of associations with people away from football. For Scott, it is important for him to feel a connectedness with others. An "I Must" activity would potentially be chatting with his parents. This was chosen because they would be able to update Scott about themselves and other family members. Thereafter as a way of practicing self-care and connectedness, an "I Can" activity would be going to church. In this way his spirituality would be nurtured and it is an important activity that will entail more connectedness. This can be followed by another "I Can," brunch with his high school buddy. Lastly, an "I Wish" would be a study group with others that would keep him aligned with his academic goals.

APPENDIX C: CJ'S ACTIVITY CHOICES—KEY

Roommate 2 Scenario: CJ, a college sophomore, has been coined as a scholar and is attending on a full academic scholarship. For him, Sundays mean digging into his studies without the hassle of attending classes. Today is Sunday, so let's help CJ plan out his day. It may be useful to know that CJ is a perfectionist and takes pride in having been on the Dean's List each semester. He knows he has been slacking on caring for himself but reasons that his attending college is contingent on maintaining high grades. He has hopes of being a veterinarian one day. How might CJ's Sunday manifesto look?

Exercise 3: CJ's Activity Choices

Choose Task	Activity	Rank Importance
	Participate in a study group (1.5 hours)	
X	Revisit notes from the week's classes (1 hour)	2
X	Complete a cardiovascular workout (1 hour)	1
X	Attend church (2 hours)	3
	Grab brunch with a high school buddy (1.5 hours)	
X	Watch an animal-based documentary (3 hours)	3
	Go grocery shopping (1 hour)	
	Check in with parents (30 minutes)	
	Register for fall classes online (15 minutes)	
	Do laundry (1.5 hours)	

Reasoning for CJ's Sunday Personal Manifesto:

Based on the information provided for this scenario, CJ places high importance on his academic endeavors. Completing an early morning cardiovascular workout is an essential "I Must" activity, as it will promote health and higher levels of mental balance. Before moving forward with the day, to keep his mind agile an "I Can" would be doing something academic. He might take some time to revisit notes from the week's classes or participate in a study group. For this instance, revisiting notes was chosen. Next Sunday, CJ may flip-flop by scheduling a tentative time to participate in a study group for the following week's "I Can." Next, as another means of self-care, an "I Wish" would be attending church to promote connectedness with his spirituality and other worshipers. It is pivotal that CJ remembers balance is important to curtail mental fatigue. Lastly, since CJ aspires to become a veterinarian, he may plan his "I Wish" to watch an early evening animal-based documentary to keep him aligned with his academic goal.

APPENDIX D: LIFE HACKS AND SCENARIOS—KEY

High School

Life Hack #1: Use the Air Mask

It is admirable that Carla wants to help her friend heal and move past her grandparent's death. The death of a loved one is especially hard to deal with. Carla may need to help her friend seek professional help and gently suggest the important life hack of taking a pause from her studies to care for herself. These steps are important for Carla to stay accountable to her goals.

Life Hack #2: Accept the Apology

David has been put in a difficult situation but has handled it well thus far. Coexisting in a class with his ex-girlfriend's ex may be uncomfortable but doable. When an opportunity presents itself he may want to consider the life hack of having a private conversation with Ron to clear the air. In this way it releases the classmate from feeling pressure and over time David could gain a true friend. David will serve himself well by learning this interpersonal skill early in life.

Life Hack #3: Own the Room

Kellie has some work to do to build her confidence but can pull it off with help. With her friends, she may want to consider some questions the panelists may ask and prepare some answers. Mock interviews with her friends would be a huge help. Lastly, Kellie needs to decide on her attire for the day of the interview. Many have found confidence in using the life hack of assuring they are wearing professional attire that fits, is clean, and is well pressed.

Life Hack #4: Room for Calm

Derek should be proud of his accomplishments. More than ever, Derek must keep his cadence. He may want to use the life hack of finding times for meditation. Derek should consider scheduling time to meditate several times per day if needed. The more often he meditates the more he will be able to take advantage of moments of calmness.

Life Hack #5: Have a Happy Zone

Brian's health has been a challenge over this last week. Now that he feels better it's important that he allots his time wisely. Studying for the test should have been his only priority today. Brian may want to do his shift and make time to study in the latter part of the day, then wake a few hours earlier in the morning to study again. Moving forward, Brian should find peace in learning a new life hack: being more conscious of putting boundaries around commitments.

Life Hack #6: Clean Eater

Omar has experienced a wake-up call. Being mature for his age, he understands the importance of making some wellness-based improvements in his life. Eating well is an individual choice. While in the high school cafeteria he can consider the healthier foods, like a grilled chicken salad with low-fat dressing. Another life hack he can use includes staying away from high sugar items such as desserts and sodas. To keep his momentum, Omar may want to read literature and articles on health basics.

Life Hack #7: Deliberate Action

Eldra is experiencing an issue many people experience. Wanting to feel accepted by her peers is a natural inclination. In this situation she seems to have been building a relationship with people she has admired from afar. She must understand there are consequences for every action. In this case, cutting school can have negative implications on several levels. Eldra needs to use the life hack of taking deliberate action to remain aligned with her academic endeavors.

Life Hack #8: Assigned Seating

Many times people feel obligated to stay attached to neutral- or negative-energy people just because of a long-standing relationship. Melody sees the need to take control of her academic progress and wants to position herself around high achievers. She can do this by taking note of people within her classes who appear to be doing well academically and learn about study groups her school may provide. For a Winner's edge, Melody should use the life hack of inquiring of her counselor about weekend college preparation courses.

Life Hack #9: Earn the Comfort

Ken is perfecting the habit of saving and the unexpected bonus helps! In his case, he wants to take some pressure off of himself by purchasing some big-ticket items he thinks he may need for college. It would be to Ken's advantage to stay focused on purchasing his computer (as planned) and continuing his habit of saving his money. For his efforts, he may want to consider using a small portion of the money to treat himself.

Life Hack #10: Come Out Swinging

Pricilla has made a mistake that many high school students make, but it is great that she has realized early that there is hope. To start, Pricilla wants to use the life hack of positioning herself around the right people and immediately limit exposure to negative and neutral energy. She should seek others who are forward-thinking and who are excelling in their studies with aspirations of moving forward and into college.

Life Hack #11: Hold the Vision

Tory has big dreams and it will take drive and ambition to accomplish these goals. Her ruthless trainer wants to see Tory succeed. His tactics may not be what Tory favors, but she must realize his tactics have worked. Victoria may want to consider the life hack of becoming mentally tough for her training sessions. Immersing herself in her trainer's way of doing business will move her closer to her goal.

Life Hack #12: Live a Simple Life

Anderson has developed the habit of saving. This habit has served him well, as he is now able to finance his own trip. Through this saving process, he now understands that the large goal is more important than minor conveniences, such as a travel pillow or new headphones. He will want to use the life hack of keeping the overall goal in the forefront of his mind and, in this way, resolve to put all his energy into his goal of attending a college out of state.

Life Hack #13: Smell Life

It is good that Carson wants to reinvent his exercise regimen. Resolving to do so with others can give him the opportunity to build interpersonal skills while practicing self-care. Within a nature-based hiking group he can gain appreciation for nature. Carson should allow his senses to run wild as he enjoys the greenery, seek the sounds of the running streams, and use the life hack of enjoying the warmth of the morning sun.

College Freshman

Life Hack #14: Be a Conversationalist

Though nervous, Harley is being presented with a golden opportunity to start a connection with a fellow classmate. This is a great way to build interpersonal skills by collecting information and sharing something about herself. The key is to resist the urge to talk too much. The name of the game is to listen. Many times, merely saying "hello" can open the door to the other person being willing to share as much as we like and more.

Life Hack #15: Be Amazed

Joslyn is in a great position to come out of her element. The challenge set by her friends will not only challenge her but also potentially introduce her to music she may actually enjoy, adding to her collection of favorite tunes. She will do well to use the life hack of doing some research about popular country singers and practicing some of their songs.

Life Hack #16: 'Tis the Season

Angel has a busy schedule trying to juggle her college courses, work, and a social life. She keeps exercise as an important part of her life. With the activities she wants to do this weekend she needs to set priorities. Maybe for weekends she can block time to study then work her weekend job. For the sake of upholding her health habits, she can complete an abbreviated workout and be extra cautious of limiting portions. Moving forward, she wants to use the invaluable life hack of being mindful of how she freely gives her time.

Life Hack #17: Warm Greetings Matter

Within Jessica's family, she has been excused from being verbal. However in college it is essential that she wraps her mind around the importance of building interpersonal skills. She can start off by resolving to share a smile with the people she encounters and be ready to have a brief conversation as people initiate conversations. Jessica can start by using the life hack of challenging herself to introduce herself and encouraging the same of others.

Life Hack #18: Laugh at Yourself

Ted made a mistake that may cost him a bit of embarrassment for some time. It was good that he took the mistake in stride and was able to move on with his day. To continue to move past the incident he may need to keep his perspective light and use the life hack of preparation. In other words, Ted may want to prepare himself for others approaching him about the incident in the future. What a way to build interpersonal skills and meet new people!

Life Hack #19: Fulfill a Duty

Being a part of a mentorship program is the gift that keeps giving. Even though Heaven's circumstances have changed, it's important that she keeps her pledge. Heaven may want to consider her schedule and use the life hack of being transparent about the capacity in which she can donate her time. If it is minimal it's OK. As time goes on Heaven can try to etch more time in her schedule at points that work best for her.

Life Hack #20: Build a Name

Kevin decided to take the class as an elective because he knows he struggles with his self-confidence. For the assignment, it would be a great time for him to write down some of his strengths or traits that may have been of benefit to others. For assistance, Kevin may want to use the life hack of talking to some of his friends, learning traits they may appreciate in him, and asking them to elaborate. These traits should be used as the foundation to sell himself during the skit.

Life Hack #21: Use Tact

Otis's friend's father putting trust in Otis to bring his son back to be with the family speaks volumes about the respect they have for Otis. The first task Otis must complete is to be sure he has a conversation with his friend in a private place. If Otis feels he needs assistance, he may want to use the life hack of seeking assistance from the experienced counselors at the college's student services center. These individuals are well trained to handle such delicate situations.

Life Hack #22: Catnap

Ivy has found it important to start a savings plan to put money away for her upcoming vacation. She is to be commended for wanting to take time for herself. However, it is important that Ivy uses the life hack of carefully balancing her part-time job with her academic obligations. To keep her priorities, Ivy needs to ensure she does not become overwhelmed. Adequate sleep and rest will serve Ivy well.

Life Hack #23: Handwritten Note

Charles is taking on a great trait early—finding gratitude. Many people wait until the holiday season to show their appreciation. Why wait? Charles can acknowledge these special people by writing a short handwritten letter or using the life hack of sending a simple thank-you card any time of the year.

Life Hack #24: Etch it in Stone

AJ needs to make some immediate improvements if he wants to pass his biology class. When presenting his plan to the professor, he will need to make a commitment to attend each class and take notes. He may want to consider linking up with fellow students and committing to writing and then implementing a concise manifesto where he devotes more study time to the class. During his study times, he may want to consider using the life hack of reviewing class notes.

Life Hack #25: Clear the Air

Michelle has a right to be disappointed with her friend for breaking her trust. Now may be the time for Michelle to break her silence and have a heart-to-heart discussion with her friend. She may want to meet her friend at a mutually agreeable time and use the life hack of letting her requirements for the friendship be known. Thereafter, they can both move on.

Life Hack #26: Cultivate Inner Peace

Morgan has always wanted to go to college and play in a band with people from different backgrounds and musical abilities. She must take the sweet with the bitter. Being around people from different backgrounds, ethnicities, and cultures gives her an opportunity to sharpen her interpersonal skills. To stay focused on her goal of learning form others while refining her craft, she should consider finding brief moments for herself. Within these brief intervals she can do quick deep-breathing exercises and meditate.

Life Hack #27: Say a Name

Erin understands her weakness and wants to make improvements. Learning and routinely using an individual's name is important in college and well beyond. Erin can start by using the life hack of privately asking her professor how to properly pronounce his name. Thereafter, she can practice writing the professor's name several times in a recognizable manner, then using his name on every occasion possible.

Life Hack #28: Something Unique

Annabella likes to keep her friends close. At this time she needs to understand the lack of communication from others is merely a coincidence. This does not mean others do not appreciate the person she is. Life happens for everyone. These are golden opportunities for her to realize she is worthy and use the life hack of investing more time and energy into her personal priorities. These may include devoting more time to her studies, enjoying a hobby, and/or considering more ways to practice self-care.

Life Hack #29: Seek Positive People

To a newly enrolled student, college can be a culture shock. However, Jasmine has what it takes to connect with new people. Some life hacks she can use may include making connections with new people by considering student-based organizations of interest around the campus and starting conversations with her classmates. Also, now may be a good time for Jasmine to start to explore volunteer-based activities.

Life Hack #30: Reclaim Your Time

Jewels's assignment was an eye-opener, as it shed light on her poor personal habits regarding social media sites. Jewels may want to uninstall social media applications from her smartphone. Lastly she may want to use the life hack of only using her laptop for limited amounts of time and viewing social media sites on the weekends only.

College Sophomore

Life Hack #31: Superfoods

It is admirable that Steve wants to spend time with friends while being accountable to his personal health goal of eating well. One life hack Steve can do to stay healthy on the road trip is to pack some nutrient-rich foods, such as bite-sized pieces of vegetables, raw fruit, and unsalted nuts (e.g., walnuts and almonds). Otherwise, during the stops to eat on the road, Steve can consider salads and other healthy choices.

Life Hack #32: The Art of Saying "No"

Douglas has been planning to have a much-needed leisure day to himself. He needs to think twice about his friend calling to make a last-minute request. If Douglas really wants to help his friend, perhaps he can use the life hack of informing the friend that he is willing to help if time allows during the latter part of the day. Otherwise they can both reschedule car shopping to another mutually agreeable time.

Life Hack #33: Start Small

Shaun has always been an ambitious person, so challenges in college are no different. There are several ways he can ensure his success in each class. It is important that Shaun has an airtight personal manifesto that includes rationing non-academic activities, retaining positive relationships, foregoing part-time work, and making inquiries of classmates who may have taken some of the courses he plans to take. Shaun would also benefit from the life hack of a self-care-based regimen to include exercise and limiting processed foods.

Life Hack #34: Rise Early

Morning classes will be new for Linda, but with some preparation she will be able to move into her new regimen with ease. Some life hacks she can use are to decompress earlier in the evening by limiting screen time and going to bed by 9 p.m. For a mental boost, it is important that she considers a quick breakfast. This could include something high in protein and a small portion of carbohydrates, with water.

Life Hack #35: Just Smile

Jesus has recognized he is out of his element. The negativity in the room could be neutralized over time if he continues to keep his energy high. He has an opportunity to embrace this moment of truth tighter by mentally preparing for the energy before each class. Jesus should use the life hack of smiling whenever possible, then only taking in the positive energy.

Life Hack #36: Gratitude

Gina knows she is fortunate that her illness will go away over time. However, she continues to pity herself. For Gina, gratitude may mean considering all the things that are going well in her life. Life hacks she can use include scheduling time to meditate before bedtime and upon rising in the morning. To minimize self-loathing, she may want to consider adding volunteerism to her personal schedule.

Life Hack #37: Develop Muscles

Brett understands the importance of self-care. Now that Brett is in a group that uses Sundays for studying, he may want to reevaluate some personal habits. For example, he may want to use Saturday as his day of rest and find a place to worship on that day. Based on his values, he may want to use the life hack of omitting himself from the study group once per month and making his intentions known.

Life Hack #38: Decompress

Marissa's intentions to stay on the soccer team are great. However, the constant anxiety she is experiencing is unhealthy. She needs to talk to the coach. If there is no resolution, she may want to talk to another member of the college staff about the issue. For now, Marissa may want to consider the life hack of finding moments to meditate as a means to escape these times.

Life Hack #39: Believe in Your System

A connection to a higher being is part of self-care. Being connected to a place of worship is a personal choice. Jack likes the people who attend the church but questions some of the teachings. A solution may be to ask questions. Jack should feel free to explore various places of worship in his leisure time. It is admirable that Jack wants to cultivate his spirituality.

Life Hack #40: Resiliency

Understandably Xavier is going through a hard time. It is essential that he takes a pause and practices self-care. This pause will allow him to regain his perspective and move forward. Xavier may want to reach out and confide in some trusted friends. Also it could be a good time to use the life hack of reaching out to a trained college counselor who has experience helping students.

College Junior

Life Hack #41: Listen to Hear

Lou and most of the others in the group appear to take pride in doing a good job. Sometimes we find others may not have the same level of zeal. It is important that Lou is clear about expectations with everyone. There could be a number of reasons the student may not be fulfilling her part of the project. Lou should consider the life hack of holding an informal conversation. For Lou, a start could be building rapport through starting a discussion about an interest unrelated to the class. Then during the next informal conversation, he can drill down to the issue within the class. Through being open to relate and hear, he may learn how he can support his fellow student.

Life Hack #42: Monday Motivation

Mary is rejuvenated and is ready to set herself up for a productive week. It is wise that she wants to use the life hack of prioritizing her time and start off on the right foot. She should start building her personal manifestos by finding blocks of time for getting involved in study groups as needed, taking advantage of office hours to confer with her professors, and practicing self-care basics.

Life Hack #43: Take Less Space

Andrew is learning lessons early in life about the value of minimizing his lifestyle. It's OK if others do not share his same viewpoint. However, it is important that a potential long-term partner has some of the same fundamental viewpoints. Andrew may want to provide some examples of how he has benefited from this lifestyle. Without being over the top, he may want to lead by using the life hack of being an example to his girlfriend and seeing where things go.

Life Hack #44: See the Lesson

Jeff has been left in a vulnerable position a few times and it has cost him. At this point, Jeff may want to consider talking to the group upon arrival at the coffee shop about how they (as a group) plan to take care of the bill. Jeff may want to consider that the group is unaware of the issue. Also, upon being served their drinks, Jeff may want to use the life hack of building his interpersonal skills by taking the initiative to request the check and immediately divide the cost evenly amongst the group.

Life Hack #45: Expand Horizons

Based on Reece's great working relationship with his supervisor, he is told about an opportunity across campus. He should be proud of his accomplishments but has reservations. This is understandable. Supervisory skills are easy to acquire if he is willing to take the time. Should he pursue and get the position, he should use the life hack of being transparent about expectations of his friends/potential subordinates.

Life Hack #46: Change the Music

Shante's desire to reassess her relationships is painfully necessary, especially when she is feeling like negative energy is having an effect on her demeanor. She will do well to use the life hack of trying to initiate upbeat conversations and change the subject when she feels the mood is going in a somber direction. If such tactics do not work, weaning her relations will serve her well.

Life Hack #47: Strength in Numbers

Jason understands public speaking is not his strong point. This is a class where he will need to put extra energy into building the confidence to speak in front of others with the help of lots of practice. It would be to his advantage to build relationships with classmates who seemingly take delight in the course. Another life hack he can use is simply asking his classmates for help.

Life Hack #48: Watch Your Dividends Grow

It is evident that Rachel needs to be more conscious about caring for herself. She needs to consider ways to practice self-care daily and promptly add them to her personal manifesto. Life hacks for personal care could include adequate rest, socialization with others, an exercise regimen several days per week, and meditation.

College Senior and Graduate School

Life Hack #49: Fuel Your Body

Don is not a night owl but in this case he has no choice. On the days Don participates in the late-night study sessions he may want to find ways to rest earlier in the evening. Maybe he can use the life hack of preparing for his 7 a.m. class before his night study session so as not to be in a rush in the morning. Also Don may want to be conscious of foods that could provide fuel needed for an extra mental boost.

Life Hack #50: Your Possible

Jacqueline is wise to take counsel from others in her family who have taken the academic journey. But with others not seeing her new ambition, this is the time to use the life hack of seeking role models who provide support and encouragement. If Jacqueline continues to listen to the well-intended naysayers, she may abandon her dreams of pursuing advanced education.

Life Hack #51: Informed Decisions

It is always a good feeling to have one's efforts acknowledged by others. To move forward in any task asked of us, it is fair to have full access to all information before making commitments. If Chris should accept this new task, he may want to ensure he is clear about his need for adequate resources (e.g., help) and time constraints of how long he plans to be involved in the endeavor.

Life Hack #52: Be Wrong

Ada is not new to creative writing, however there is a lot she could learn within the course. From the beginning Ada has noticed some conflicts, but is well positioned to gain a wealth of knowledge from someone who has had formal training in the writing field. Ada would do well to mentally position herself as a newbie and use the life hack of having an open mind to learn as much as possible, which will perfect her craft.

Life Hack #53: Brick by Brick

Augustine has made some great accomplishments in the fashion industry thus far. Even at a young age, others have taken note of her talent. Though she may not be completely confident in her abilities, this is not the time to shrink away. Based on her talent she has been called to duty. To gain a winning edge and build her confidence, she may want to use the life hack of doing some research about the president's fashion sense. Thus, she can come to the meeting with some suggestions and start to build interpersonal skills with individuals in positions of power.

Life Hack #54: Stand on Shoulders

Marlene has always had admiration for her uncle. Though some time has passed, it is never too late to reconnect. Perhaps before the family reunion, she can use the life hack of calling her uncle and planning to meet at a mutually agreeable time while she is in town. This would be a great way to not only catch up but to gain some new insight along with encouragement. It is important to show homage to those people who have helped us along the way.

Life Hack #55: Be Choosy

Christina has built quite a reputation for herself, as she takes pride in devoting large amounts of time to socialize with her friends. However, since she wants to put more time and effort into her studies, she needs to ration her time. A life hack she may want to consider is making fewer dates but invite several friends at once. This will decrease time away from her studies and keep her desire to stay connected to others alive.

Life Hack #56: Power of Touch

Luz's assignment has put her in a position to help others. Her advocacy work has started off abruptly, but she will learn valuable tools over the course of her assignments. It's important that Luz sticks to the books and uses the principles she acquired in training. Using the life hacks of showing empathy through a hug (as appropriate) and/or simply listening serve her well.

Life Hack #57: New Genre

Graduation time can be high pressure, especially when one's ideas of a celebration differ from others'. Taylor has been gifted with a family who appreciates music. Taylor should use the life hack of approaching her family about her wishes. Especially if she approaches them with gratitude and open-mindedness. This may be a great way to start a conversation about her preferences and her must-haves. Most likely her family wants her to have her special day her way.

Life Hack #58: Be Joyous

Not everyone is a morning person and Lisa is learning this lesson the hard way. After Lisa has noticed the trend, she needs to put boundaries around conserving positive energy in her life. Lisa can start by one evening explaining her morning regimen to her roommate and why it is important to her. Thereafter Lisa may want to use the life hack of sharing ways to practice self-care in the morning. If the roommate does not follow suit she will at least understand and hopefully respect Lisa's routine.

Life Hack #59: Right a Wrong

Dean has carried around misdirected animosity for some time. Now that he knows the truth, it is time that he takes the weight off his shoulders and has a conversation with his ex-teammate. Dean can consider directly approaching the teammate to simply apologize. Also Dean may want to consider using the life hack of writing a short and concise handwritten note.

Life Hack #60: Walk Among the Runners

Vivian has developed the invaluable habit of getting adequate sleep. This may be the time for Vivian to try something new that seems to work for others. It may be to her advantage to plan her schedule around the time the study group meets up. Since adequate sleep is a concern, Vivian may want to consider taking a power nap before the meet-up and drinking plenty of water to stay vibrant. Also she may want to use the life hack of making her intentions known too, by only committing herself to meeting a few times a week or as needed.

APPENDIX E: COMPILATION OF THE WINNER'S CREED

The Winner's Creed for Moments of Truth:

- Winners learn most people's experience in academia is life changing, to a certain extent.
- Winners learn that iron sharpens iron—surround ourselves with the most positive energy conducive to winning.
- Winners learn moments of truth that build sustainable relationships come in spurts and are rarely convenient.
- Winners learn that by thoughtfully handling each scenario, we strengthen our interpersonal skills.

The Winner's Creed for Paying Dues:

- Winners learn that success in high school heightens the probability of successful outcomes in higher learning.
- Winners learn we pay now or pay later.
- Winners learn college doors swing wide open for the ambitious student with the desire to win in higher learning.
- Winners learn developing strategies to take ownership in our journey develops accountability and keeps our "why" in plain view.

The Winner's Creed for Speaking of Degrees:

- Winners learn today's brick-and-mortar college campus has everything we need to achieve academic success.
- Winners learn the higher the level of education one pursues, the more rigorous the curriculum becomes.
- Winners learn after reviewing our goals, we can go as fast or as slow as we prefer.

The Winner's Creed for Seeking Support

- Winners learn the bigger the goal the crazier it could and absolutely should look.
- Winners learn to never underestimate the power of making an inquiry.
- Winners learn how to seek the support of others and also know that our interpersonal skills are traits worth developing early.
- Winners learn to lend a hand and be of service to others within our circle of support and elsewhere.

The Winner's Creed for Planning Around Other People

- Winners learn the notion that we have all day to accomplish something can derail our goals.
- Winners learn that having relationships in our everyday lives can leave us susceptible to helping and supporting other people as they too support us.
- Winners learn when last-minute requests are made of us from friends, it is OK to tactfully decline (as warranted).
- Winners learn that friends may be a little disappointed about the lack of expediency on our part, however true friends will respect our boundaries.
- Winners learn to use the life hack of *under-promising but over-delivering*.

The Winner's Creed for Breaks and Reward Systems

- Winners learn taking a momentary break helps us remain affixed to our "why."
- Winners learn pauses are good around periods of high stress, such as studying for final exams and managing sudden life-altering events.
- Winners learn sickness and/or deaths in our lives cannot be anticipated, even with our best planning skills.
- Winners learn a reward system gives us something to look forward to as we are in the midst of our busy lives.

The Winner's Creed for Developing a Manifesto:

- ♟ Winners learn cultivating the practice of being organized and building a written daily manifesto, or personal plan, to manage our college schedule allows us to keep a running record of all our goals.
- ♟ Winners learn through trial and error to stay mindful of the most mentally agile moments of the day.
- ♟ Winners learn balance cultivates self-care while allowing us to keep integrity with our limited stores of time and energy.

The Winner's Creed for Life Hacks for Channeling Energy

- ♟ Winners learn all people have energy.
- ♟ Winners learn there is no substitute for being around uplifting individuals who aspire to positively impact others and themselves.
- ♟ Winners learn to be vigilant of not allowing too much neutral energy within our environment, as neutral energy is simply dead weight.
- ♟ Winners learn it is OK to put boundaries around what kind of energy we deem as acceptable and unacceptable in our lives by repositioning the seating chart.

The Winner's Creed for Life Hacks for Nurturing the Body

- ♟ Winners learn stress is unavoidable.
- ♟ Winners learn fresher foods with limited ingredients are instant sources of energy to promote mental clarity.
- ♟ Winners learn that these days, people are reaping the benefits of superfoods.
- ♟ Winners learn that high-quality foods can be found in the college campus cafeteria.

APPENDIX F: COMPILATION OF MOTIVATIONAL AFFIRMATIONS

A pilot told me that some of the big jet airplanes have a series of blades extending down the wings which cause air to swirl toward the rear of the plane. This provides the necessary turbulence for directional accuracy in flight. If the air is too smooth, some roughness has to be added to improve flight conditions. Perhaps suffering and hardship serve the same purpose for a human being. Maybe we need "turbulence" to help us develop a sense of direction so that we may ultimately reach the destination intended for us in life.

—Norman Vincent Peale

Education is the most powerful weapon which you can use to change the world.

—Nelson Mandela

I have never let my schooling interfere with my education.

—Mark Twain

The most important single ingredient in success is knowing how to get along with people.

—Theodore Roosevelt

The thing about paying your dues is that you're not the one who sets the price.

—Alan Robert Neal

Whatever the mind can conceive and believe, it can achieve.

—Napoleon Hill

Each one teach one.

—African American Proverb

If you fail to plan, you are planning to fail.

—Benjamin Franklin

There is virtue in work and there is virtue in rest. Use both and overlook neither.

—Alan Cohen

Goals are the links in the chain that connect activity to accomplishment.

—Tom Ziglar

A person's energy can tell you more about them than their own word.

—Anonymous

You are what you eat.

—Unknown

It's possible.

—Les Brown

Bonus Affirmations

Being realistic is the most commonly traveled road to mediocrity.

—Will Smith

You are the designer of your destiny; you are the author of your story.

—Lisa Nichols

It is not what we get. But who we become, what we contribute…that gives meaning to our lives.

—Tony Robbins

Fall in love with the process and results will come.

—Eric Thomas

If you don't have a mountain, build one and then climb it. And after you climb it, build another one; otherwise you start to flatline in your life.

—Sylvester Stallone

Success is liking yourself, liking what you do, and liking how you do it.

—Maya Angelou

I'm not saying I'm gonna…change the world but I guarantee that I will spark the brain that will change the world.

—Tupac Amaru Shakur

The world is a dangerous place to live, not because of the people who are evil, but because of the people who don't do anything about it.

—Albert Einstein

We are all self-made, but only the successful will admit it.

—Earl Nightingale

If you are going to achieve excellence in big things, you develop the habit in little matters. Excellence is not an exception, it's a prevailing attitude.

—Colin Powell

The coward dies a thousand deaths, the brave but one.

—Ernest Hemingway
paraphrasing
William Shakespeare

WINNER'S CIRCLE WORKSPACE

WINNER'S CIRCLE WORKSPACE

About the Author

As a Pittsburgh, Pennsylvania native, Dr. Anika Thrower obtained her undergraduate degree in nutrition from Norfolk State University. Later she was awarded both a masters and doctorate degree in public health from Walden University. Because of her exemplary research, Walden University presented her with the prestigious Presidential Alumni Research Dissemination Award.

Dr. Thrower is a health-based adjunct faculty member with Springfield College, teaching both undergraduate and graduate coursework. She has taken delight in mentoring and overseeing hundreds of students. Through her curricula she interweaves the importance of today's college-minded students keeping their health status a priority while maintaining their cadence on their journey in higher learning. Dr. Thrower is also known as the Self-Preservationist, as she encourages each student to add grit to their "why" in an effort to remain forward-moving.

Utilizing over 15 years of expertise, Dr. Thrower has published a collage of peer-reviewed scholarly articles around wellness. She has served in various underserved populations around the United States, including a Native American community. In addition to being a health-based writer for over a decade, Dr. Thrower served as the Co-Chair of the New Haven Food Policy Council (NHFPC). She is proud to be a contributing member of the City of New Haven's first Food Action Plan. Dr. Thrower has been a health-based contributing writer for a newspaper entitled *An African American Point of View*, which is distributed at over 16,000 locations throughout Massachusetts and Connecticut.

Dr. Thrower's passion for people improving their respective health outcomes has led her to become a wellness expert within government-funded programs. She has extensive expertise in utilizing science-based health models to impact healthy lifestyle behaviors in the lives of thousands of families. Endorsed by the Connecticut Department of Public Health (and the first health care center in the State of Connecticut) as a principle researcher, she critically examined health behaviors and a scientific behavior model to determine predictors of poor health statuses.

Outside of poor dietary choices and health habits, as other scholarly resources suggest, a key finding of Dr. Thrower's investigation uncovered that a low rate of educational attainment heightened poor health outcomes among minorities.

As a thought leader, Dr. Thrower's assertion is that higher learning is the gateway to communities generationally experiencing higher qualities of life.

In her leisure, she enjoys coffee shops, traveling, and meditation.

www.ingramcontent.com/pod-product-compliance
Lightning Source LLC
Chambersburg PA
CBHW081426090426
42740CB00017B/3202